Data Governance in Healthcare IT

Siranjeevi Dheenadhayalan

1

Data Governance in Healthcare IT

Ensuring Compliance and Privacy in Medical Data Management

Siranjeevi Dheenadhayalan
Author and Software Product Manager

Table of Contents

Chapter 1: Introduction to Data Governance in Healthcare IT

In the ever-evolving landscape of healthcare, the management and integrity of data stand at the forefront of operational efficiency and patient care improvement. The complex nature of healthcare data, which encompasses electronic health records (EHRs), billing information, patient demographics, clinical research, and more, necessitates a robust framework for governance to ensure that data is accurate, secure, and utilized effectively. As healthcare organizations continue to embrace digital transformation, the importance of comprehensive data governance strategies cannot be overstated.

Data governance refers to the processes, policies, and standards that govern how data is collected, managed, and utilized within an organization. In healthcare, effective data governance serves multiple critical functions: it ensures compliance with regulatory mandates, safeguards patient privacy, and enhances the ability to leverage data analytics for improved decision-making and outcomes. As the healthcare sector increasingly confronts challenges related to data breaches, interoperability issues, and the need for transparency, the implementation of structured data governance frameworks has emerged as a key priority.

Establishing a data governance framework in healthcare requires a multi-faceted approach that takes into account the unique characteristics of the industry. One critical aspect is the diverse nature of stakeholders involved, which includes healthcare providers, payers, patients, and regulatory bodies. Each stakeholder has varying interests in the data, demanding a collaborative approach to governance that fosters transparency and accountability. This necessitates the formation of interdisciplinary teams tasked with defining governance policies, establishing data stewardship roles, and ensuring adherence to standards.

The rise of interoperability in healthcare also underscores the significance of data governance. With the shift toward integrated care models and health information exchanges, it is essential that data is not only accurate but also readily available across different systems and platforms. Poor data quality can lead to miscommunication between healthcare providers, ultimately compromising patient safety and leading to adverse outcomes. A data governance framework emphasizes data quality management, setting standards for data entry, validation, and maintenance, thereby enhancing the reliability of data exchanged among different healthcare entities.

Compliance with regulatory frameworks, such as the Health Insurance Portability and Accountability Act (HIPAA) and the 21st Century Cures Act, is a pivotal element of data governance. These regulations impose strict requirements on how patient information is handled, transmitted, and stored, creating a need for healthcare organizations to have clear data governance policies in place. Failure to comply with these regulations can result in significant financial penalties and loss of trust from patients, emphasizing the importance of establishing a culture of compliance.

Equally important is the protection of patient privacy and sensitive health information. The increasing prevalence of cyber threats necessitates that data governance frameworks include robust security measures to safeguard against data breaches. Organizations must employ advanced analytics to monitor data access and usage, ensuring that only authorized personnel can interact with sensitive information. Efforts to educate all staff members on the significance of data security and the importance of adhering to governance policies are essential to fostering a culture of privacy and security within the healthcare setting.

As healthcare organizations increasingly adopt data analytics and artificial intelligence (AI) technologies, the implications of governance become even more profound. Without a solid governance framework, there is a risk of generating biased or inadequate treatment decisions based on flawed data analysis. Ensuring data integrity is imperative for deriving actionable insights that can guide clinical decisions, improve patient outcomes, and enhance operational efficiencies. Furthermore, data governance helps in the ethical use of data analytics, supporting initiatives for equitable health care delivery across diverse populations.

An effective data governance strategy also incorporates data lifecycle management, encompassing the comprehensive management of data from its creation to its deletion. This includes data classification, retention policies, and archiving protocols. By understanding the lifecycle of data, healthcare organizations can make informed decisions about how data is collected, stored, and shared, ensuring that it is not only available for necessary purposes but also protected from unnecessary access or exposure.

The move toward value-based care and population health management highlights the urgent need for data governance that supports outcome-based measurements. By leveraging data governance practices, organizations can better track performance, assess outcomes, and implement evidence-based strategies that improve patient care. This involves creating frameworks for measuring quality indicators and sharing results transparently with stakeholders, ultimately driving continuous improvement in healthcare delivery.

In conclusion, the integration of effective data governance within healthcare IT systems is instrumental in addressing the challenges posed by rapid technological advancements and evolving regulatory landscapes. From establishing strong data stewardship to ensuring compliance and enhancing data quality, a well-designed governance framework enables healthcare organizations to harness the full potential of their data assets. As the industry continues to advance, prioritizing data governance not only protects patient information but also serves as a cornerstone for innovation and quality improvement in healthcare delivery. Through committed governance practices, healthcare providers can transform data into a strategic asset, driving better outcomes and elevating the standard of care for patients.

1.1 Definition and Importance of Data Governance

Data governance in healthcare IT constitutes a comprehensive framework that establishes the management, usage, quality, and security of data across healthcare organizations. It encompasses policies, procedures, and standards that dictate how data is created, stored, shared, and utilized. At its core, data governance serves as an essential mechanism to ensure that critical health information is accurate, timely, and accessible to relevant stakeholders while also safeguarding patient privacy and complying with regulatory mandates.

The significance of data governance in the healthcare sector cannot be overstated. Healthcare organizations are inundated with vast amounts of data originating from various sources such as electronic health records (EHRs), lab results, clinical trials, patient surveys, and billing systems. Proper data governance ensures that this data is not only well-organized but also capitalized upon to enhance patient care, optimize operational efficiencies, and drive informed decision-making.

One primary aspect of data governance is the establishment of data quality standards. High-quality data is foundational to effective healthcare delivery; it enables clinicians to make sound diagnostic and treatment decisions. Poor data quality can result in inaccuracies that undermine patient care, including medication errors and misdiagnoses. Consequently, data governance emphasizes the importance of data accuracy, consistency, completeness, and timeliness, implementing protocols for data validation and quality control.

Compliance with healthcare regulations—including the Health Insurance Portability and Accountability Act (HIPAA) and the Health Information Technology for Economic and Clinical

Health (HITECH) Act—further highlights the critical need for effective data governance. These regulations impose stringent requirements on how healthcare entities manage sensitive patient information. Data governance frameworks incorporate compliance measures to protect patient confidentiality and data integrity, thus minimizing the risk of legal repercussions and enhancing organizational credibility.

In the context of healthcare IT, data governance also establishes clear roles and responsibilities related to data management. This involves the creation of data stewardship roles, where designated individuals or teams are tasked with overseeing specific data domains. By defining ownership and accountability, data governance mitigates the risks associated with data mismanagement and empowers healthcare organizations to leverage data responsibly and ethically.

The governance framework facilitates standardized data definitions across the organization. In a typical healthcare environment, various departments may utilize the same terms or metrics differently, leading to inconsistencies in data interpretation. A unified data governance strategy delineates a common vocabulary, ensuring that all stakeholders have a shared understanding of key metrics. This standardization is pivotal in achieving operational efficiencies and accurate reporting and analytics.

Moreover, data governance is instrumental in fostering a culture of data-driven decision-making throughout healthcare organizations. When staff members understand the importance and utilization of data governance, they are more likely to engage in practices that uphold data quality and security. Continuous training and communication around governance policies can cultivate an environment where data is not merely an afterthought but rather a pivotal resource for clinical and operational excellence.

Another critical dimension of data governance is the empowerment of analytical capabilities. In an era characterized by the proliferation of big data and advanced analytical tools, healthcare organizations are increasingly focusing on extracting actionable insights from their data repositories. A robust data governance framework ensures that the necessary data is available, accessible, and reliable for advanced analytics initiatives. This enables organizations to engage in predictive modeling, clinical decision support, and population health management, ultimately leading to improved patient outcomes and resource allocation strategies.

Additionally, data governance provides a blueprint for effective data lifecycle management. Data does not merely exist in a vacuum; it lives through distinct phases—from collection and storage to archival and deletion. Well-defined governance policies map out the procedures concerning data retention and disposal, thereby managing storage costs while conforming to regulatory mandates. This oversight is especially critical in healthcare, where the improper disposal of sensitive information can lead to significant breaches of patient trust and legal challenges.

Technical integration, particularly relevant in a digitally transforming healthcare landscape, is another area where data governance plays a crucial role. Standardized protocols and procedures are necessary to ensure that different systems and platforms can communicate effectively. A cohesive data governance strategy enables healthcare entities to achieve interoperability, thereby facilitating secure data exchange among healthcare providers, payers, and patients.

The importance of data governance in healthcare extends beyond mere compliance and risk management; it is integral to enhancing patient safety and quality of care. By ensuring that data is accurate, timely, and securely accessed, providers can make more informed clinical decisions that ultimately lead to better health outcomes.

In conclusion, the definition and importance of data governance in healthcare IT are multifaceted. As healthcare organizations increasingly harness the volume and complexity of data, the need for rigorous governance practices becomes paramount. The establishment of robust data governance not only enhances data quality and compliance but also cultivates a culture of accountability, fosters analytical prowess, and ultimately drives improved patient care and organizational success. Through the lens of data governance, healthcare organizations have an opportunity to transform data into a strategic asset that underpins their mission of delivering high-quality, patient-centered care.

1.2 Regulatory Landscape Overview

In the realm of healthcare IT, data governance has emerged as a critical infrastructure for ensuring the integrity, security, and usability of health data. The regulatory landscape surrounding healthcare data governance is multifaceted, shaped by a blend of federal laws, state regulations, and industry standards that aim to protect patient information while facilitating the flow of data necessary for medical care and innovation. Understanding this complicated regulatory framework is essential for healthcare organizations seeking to implement effective data governance strategies.

At the federal level in the United States, the Health Insurance Portability and Accountability Act (HIPAA) is arguably the cornerstone of healthcare data governance. Enacted in 1996, HIPAA established national standards for the protection of sensitive patient information. Its Privacy Rule restricts the use and disclosure of protected health information (PHI), while the Security Rule delineates the safeguards that must be in place to protect electronic PHI (ePHI). Under HIPAA, entities such as healthcare providers, payers, and business associates are required to adopt administrative, physical, and technical safeguards to ensure data confidentiality, integrity, and availability. Failure to comply with HIPAA can lead to hefty fines and legal implications, making it a fundamental element of data governance strategies in healthcare organizations.

In addition to HIPAA, the Health Information Technology for Economic and Clinical Health (HITECH) Act of 2009 introduced additional provisions that extended the reach of HIPAA by promoting the adoption of electronic health records (EHR) and enhancing enforcement mechanisms. HITECH mandated that breaches of unsecured PHI be reported, creating a culture of accountability around data management. Furthermore, it incentivized the meaningful use of EHR systems, thereby fostering the growth of digital data within the healthcare sector. As such, organizations must be aware that their data governance practices must not only protect but also facilitate the effective use of electronic data to improve patient care.

The regulatory landscape does not stop at HIPAA and HITECH. The 21st Century Cures Act, enacted in 2016, aims to accelerate medical product development and bring new innovations to market more efficiently. Among its provisions is the requirement for health IT developers to ensure interoperability of electronic health systems and to prohibit information blocking practices. These regulations necessitate that healthcare organizations adopt governance practices that promote data sharing and accessibility while adhering to stringent security protocols. This balancing act alters the data governance priorities, focusing on collaborative data use while maintaining rigorous privacy standards.

State laws also contribute significantly to the regulatory environment for data governance. Many states have implemented their own privacy laws that can impose stricter regulations than HIPAA. For instance, California's Consumer Privacy Act (CCPA) gives consumers greater control over their personal information, and similar legislative frameworks are emerging across the country. Healthcare organizations operating in multiple states must navigate these varying legislative environments, which complicates their governance frameworks. Therefore, it becomes imperative for organizations to develop a comprehensive understanding of both federal and state regulations to ensure compliance.

Moreover, the rise of telehealth and mobile health applications further complicates the regulatory landscape. As these technologies proliferate, new challenges arise regarding data privacy, consent, and security. Regulatory bodies are increasingly focused on establishing guidelines that address the unique dimensions of telehealth, such as informed consent for remote patient monitoring and the secure transmission of health information over various platforms. Healthcare IT professionals must stay abreast of these developments, as failure to comply with emerging regulations can lead to significant risks related to data breaches or patient privacy violations.

Industry standards also play a pivotal role in shaping data governance best practices within healthcare IT. Organizations such as the Health Level Seven International (HL7) and the International Organization for Standardization (ISO) provide frameworks and standards for data exchange, interoperability, and information management. Adoption of these standards can improve the quality and reliability of health data, thus supporting effective governance practices. By aligning with standardized protocols, organizations can enhance their data interoperability endeavors while ensuring compliance with both regulatory and clinical needs.

Looking beyond compliance, the regulatory landscape increasingly emphasizes data stewardship, data quality, and ethical data use. The emerging focus on health equity has led to calls for organizations to ensure that data governance frameworks account for various social determinants of health. This shift necessitates not only adherence to existing regulations but also the ethical consideration of how data is collected, analyzed, and utilized. Organizations that proactively embrace this dimension of governance can foster trust with patients and stakeholders while simultaneously enhancing the value derived from health data.

In summary, navigating the regulatory landscape of healthcare IT data governance requires a dynamic and multifaceted approach. By understanding the complexities of federal laws like HIPAA, HITECH, and the 21st Century Cures Act, in addition to state regulations and industry standards, healthcare organizations can create robust governance frameworks. These frameworks will not only ensure compliance but also enhance the overall integrity, security, and usability of health data. As the healthcare IT environment continues to evolve, so too will the regulatory imperatives governing it. Organizations must thus remain vigilant and adaptable in their governance practices to meet the challenges and opportunities of a data-driven healthcare ecosystem.

1.3 Challenges in Healthcare Data Management

In the dynamic landscape of healthcare IT, data management plays a pivotal role in driving improvements in patient care and operational efficiency. However, healthcare organizations face significant challenges in effectively managing their data. These challenges can arise from a variety of sources, including technological complexity, regulatory compliance requirements, data interoperability issues, and the need to maintain patient privacy. Addressing these challenges is crucial for the advancement of data governance frameworks in healthcare.

One of the foremost challenges in healthcare data management is the sheer volume and variety of data generated daily. Health data comes from diverse sources, such as electronic health records (EHRs), wearable devices, laboratory systems, and medical imaging technologies. This multifaceted nature of data often leads to data silos, where information is trapped within specific departments or systems. The challenge of integrating this varied data into a cohesive, comprehensive format prevents healthcare organizations from gaining a holistic view of patient information and outcomes. Moreover, the lack of standardized data formats further complicates the interoperability required for seamless data sharing across different systems and providers.

Interoperability remains a persistent headache in healthcare IT. Many organizations utilize legacy systems that are not designed to communicate effectively with newer technologies. As healthcare institutions invest in upgrading their IT infrastructure, aligning disparate systems with different data standards becomes a significant hurdle. Inconsistent terminologies and definitions further exacerbate this issue, posing risks to patient safety and quality of care. Efficient data governance practices must incorporate protocols for standardizing data formats and ensuring that systems can communicate effectively, thus paving the way for a more integrated healthcare ecosystem.

Regulatory compliance represents another formidable challenge in the domain of healthcare data management. Adherence to regulations such as the Health Insurance Portability and Accountability Act (HIPAA), the Health Information Technology for Economic and Clinical Health (HITECH) Act, and other state and federal laws is paramount to safeguarding patient data. These regulations impose stringent requirements for data security, privacy, and access, which healthcare organizations must navigate carefully. With the rise in cybersecurity threats, the importance of compliance has intensified, compelling healthcare providers to regularly audit their data management practices and invest in advanced security measures. Non-compliance can lead to devastating financial penalties, irreparable reputational damage, and loss of patient trust, emphasizing the importance of robust data governance frameworks.

Furthermore, the ethical considerations surrounding healthcare data management pose a critical challenge. Healthcare organizations must balance the need for data collection with patient privacy rights, ensuring transparency and ethical use of sensitive health information. The deployment of machine learning algorithms and artificial intelligence in clinical decision-making further complicates this ethical landscape. While these technologies hold the potential to enhance patient outcomes, they also raise concerns around data bias, informed consent, and accountability for decisions made based on algorithmic predictions. Establishing clear guidelines and ethical frameworks within data governance practices is essential to address these concerns and foster trust among patients and stakeholders.

In addition to technical and regulatory hurdles, cultural challenges within healthcare organizations can hinder effective data management. A culture that prioritizes data-driven decision-making is essential for harnessing the full potential of healthcare data. Resistance to change can stem from entrenched practices and skepticism about the utility of data analytics in improving patient outcomes. Training and education on the importance of data governance and the role of data in enhancing care can help foster a more data-centric culture. Engaging leadership and staff at all levels to champion data governance initiatives is crucial in overcoming cultural resistance and promoting a collective commitment to effective data management.

Moreover, the issue of data quality cannot be overlooked in the context of healthcare data management. High-quality data is a prerequisite for informed decision-making, accurate reporting, and effective operational processes. Poor data quality can stem from various sources, including human error during data entry, lack of data validation processes, and outdated legacy systems. Regular audits and data cleaning processes must be implemented as part of a comprehensive data governance strategy to ensure that the data used across the organization is reliable and accurate. Investing in technologies that enhance data quality, such as automated validation tools and advanced analytics, can significantly reduce the risks associated with poor data management.

Finally, the advent of big data analytics and real-time data processing introduces yet another layer of complexity to healthcare data management. While the promise of big data lies in its potential to revolutionize patient care through predictive analytics and personalized medicine, the sheer scale of data generated can overwhelm existing infrastructure. Organizations need to develop scalable data management frameworks that can adapt to the increasing complexity and volume of data. Implementing efficient data governance structures will facilitate the necessary integration and analysis of big data, ultimately leading to improved patient outcomes and healthcare efficiency.

The challenges inherent in healthcare data management are multi-faceted and demand a strategic approach to data governance. By addressing issues related to data volume, interoperability, compliance, privacy, organizational culture, data quality, and scalability, healthcare organizations can better harness the power of their data. Effective data governance is not merely a regulatory necessity but a critical enabler of enhanced patient care, operational efficiency, and improved health outcomes in an increasingly data-driven healthcare landscape.

Chapter 2: Regulatory Frameworks Impacting Healthcare Data

The interplay between healthcare data governance and regulatory frameworks shapes the landscape of health information management, influencing not only compliance but also the quality of care delivered. A well-structured regulatory environment is crucial in safeguarding patient data, promoting interoperability, and fostering innovation while maintaining ethical standards.

The Health Insurance Portability and Accountability Act (HIPAA), enacted in 1996, stands at the forefront of healthcare data governance in the United States. It introduced a set of standards to protect sensitive patient information, mandating the secure handling and transmission of healthcare data. HIPAA's Privacy Rule delineates patient rights and stipulates the circumstances under which health information can be disclosed. The Security Rule supplements these provisions by instituting requirements for safeguarding electronic protected health information (ePHI) through administrative, physical, and technical safeguards. Compliance with HIPAA is non-negotiable; violating its provisions can result in substantial penalties and damages to an organization's reputation.

Beyond HIPAA, the 21st Century Cures Act has introduced additional layers of governance aimed at enhancing patient access to health information. This legislation emphasizes the importance of interoperability in healthcare IT, driving the development of open APIs (Application Programming Interfaces) that facilitate the seamless exchange of data across different systems. This act not only aims to empower patients but also encourages healthcare providers and developers to collaborate in creating solutions that provide smoother access to health data while adhering to stringent data privacy standards.

The advent of the General Data Protection Regulation (GDPR) in the European Union has also significantly influenced global healthcare data governance practices. While GDPR is broader in scope, its principles have led organizations worldwide to rethink data protection strategies. Key tenets, such as data minimization and the right to erasure (the "right to be forgotten"), necessitate that healthcare organizations be vigilant about how they collect, store, and process personal data. GDPR's emphasis on informed consent aligns closely with the ethos of patient autonomy in healthcare, reinforcing the necessity of transparent data management practices that prioritize patient rights.

Regulatory frameworks in healthcare data governance are further complicated by the emergence of technologies such as artificial intelligence (AI) and machine learning (ML). While these technologies offer substantial potential for improving patient outcomes, they also pose unique challenges related to data privacy, bias, and accountability. The lack of a comprehensive regulatory guide specifically tailored for AI in healthcare has led to calls for more defined policies that ensure ethical practices in data usage. Organizations must navigate the regulatory landscape thoughtfully, balancing innovation with ethical considerations to maintain trust with patients and stakeholders.

Telehealth, which gained unprecedented traction during the COVID-19 pandemic, has prompted regulatory adaptations to support remote care delivery. The relaxation of certain HIPAA requirements during the public health emergency facilitated rapid adoption of telehealth services; however, it also necessitated a reevaluation of data governance practices to ensure patient confidentiality and data integrity. Organizations are now tasked with implementing robust policies that anticipate the complexities introduced by telehealth technologies while remaining compliant with both existing regulations and emerging guidelines.

Data governance in healthcare is incomplete without considering the implications of organizational culture and staff training. Regulatory requirements are just one component of an organization's data management strategy. A culture of compliance must permeate every level, complemented by training programs that equip employees with the knowledge and skills necessary to uphold data privacy and security standards. This human element is often overlooked, yet it plays a pivotal role in safeguarding sensitive healthcare data and ensuring that regulatory frameworks are effectively operationalized within health organizations.

Moreover, the regulatory landscape is continually evolving, driven by technological advancements, public health necessities, and societal demands for transparency and accountability. Organizations must adopt a proactive stance, regularly updating their data governance practices to align with new regulatory directives. This includes staying abreast of evolving laws and regulations at both state and federal levels, as well as guidance from regulatory bodies such as the Office for Civil Rights (OCR) in the U.S. Department of Health and Human Services (HHS).

Emerging challenges such as ransomware attacks and data breaches further underscore the importance of maintaining robust data governance practices consistent with regulatory frameworks. The need for organizations to demonstrate due diligence in protecting patient data goes beyond compliance; it is essential for maintaining public trust and delivering high-quality healthcare. As the tension between data sharing for innovation and stringent privacy laws continues to grow, healthcare organizations must find ways to harmonize these competing interests through strategic data governance initiatives.

In conclusion, the integration of regulatory frameworks into healthcare data governance is not merely a matter of compliance, but a fundamental aspect of delivering high-quality care in a rapidly changing landscape. Organizations must embrace a culture of accountability and responsiveness, actively engaging with regulatory developments while prioritizing patient rights and ethical data stewardship. As they navigate these complexities, healthcare organizations stand to enhance their operational resilience and contribute positively to the broader ecosystem, ultimately supporting more informed and empowered patients.

2.1 Health Insurance Portability and Accountability Act (HIPAA)

The Health Insurance Portability and Accountability Act (HIPAA) stands as a seminal piece of legislation in the United States healthcare landscape, primarily established to enhance the portability and accountability of health insurance coverage while simultaneously safeguarding the confidentiality and security of patients' health information. The act was enacted in 1996, laying the groundwork for a framework that addresses both privacy rights and the administration of health information, profoundly impacting healthcare information technology (IT) and data governance practices.

At the core of HIPAA are its standards for the protection of individually identifiable health information, primarily included in the Privacy and Security Rules. The Privacy Rule delineates the permissible uses and disclosures of health information under the control of covered entities, which include healthcare providers, health plans, and certain clearinghouses. It empowers patients with rights to access their own health information and mandates providers to ensure that patient data is shared only with authorized individuals or entities. From a data governance perspective, this stipulation reinforces the importance of implementing robust data management practices that prioritize patient confidentiality and ethical considerations in health data sharing.

Equally vital is the Security Rule, which sets forth standards to protect electronic protected health information (ePHI). This includes guidance on administrative, physical, and technical safeguards. The rule mandates that organizations conduct risk assessments to identify potential vulnerabilities in their healthcare IT systems. Such assessments are critical for ensuring that appropriate safeguards are in place to protect sensitive patient data from unauthorized access and data breaches, thus underscoring the significance of a well-defined data governance strategy within healthcare organizations.

As healthcare IT systems have evolved, so too have the challenges posed by ensuring compliance with HIPAA regulations. With the advent of electronic health records (EHRs), telemedicine, and mobile health applications, the lines between accessibility and privacy have increasingly blurred. While these technologies enhance patient care and streamline operations, they also open avenues for potential misuse of health information. Thus, data governance in healthcare IT must extend beyond mere compliance to integrate a culture of accountability where the ethical use of data is prioritized.

Organizations are investing significantly in training and educating their workforce on HIPAA regulations, not only to ensure compliance but also to foster an organizational ethos of data stewardship. Such training programs are crucial in informing employees about their responsibilities related to data privacy and security, thereby minimizing human error—the leading cause of data breaches in healthcare. A culture that embraces accountability in data management fosters an environment where staff members are vigilant and proactive in safeguarding health information.

Moreover, the implementation of advanced technologies, including artificial intelligence (AI) and machine learning (ML), offers both opportunities and challenges in the context of HIPAA compliance. While these technologies can enhance patient outcomes by providing predictive analytics and personalized treatment options, they also raise complex questions around data privacy and ethical considerations. For instance, training AI algorithms on health data requires stringent adherence to HIPAA guidelines to ensure that personal health information remains protected. Therefore, data governance frameworks must adapt to incorporate these technological advancements while maintaining compliance with legal standards.

Breaches of HIPAA regulations can prove costly, with financial penalties escalating based on the severity and intentionality of the violation. The Department of Health and Human Services (HHS) Office for Civil Rights (OCR) actively enforces compliance and has undertaken numerous investigations, leading to settlements in the millions. Such regulatory scrutiny not only highlights the importance of adhering to HIPAA standards but also underscores the necessity for robust data governance protocols in healthcare IT. Organizations must remain vigilant about evolving regulations and invest in technologies that enhance data protection.

Furthermore, the advent of patient-generated health data (PGHD) introduces another layer of complexity to HIPAA compliance and data governance. As patients engage more actively in their healthcare through mobile applications and wearable devices, they generate vast amounts of health data that often intertwine with institutional data. This shift compels healthcare organizations to rethink their data governance strategies, ensuring that they address the privacy and security concerns associated with PGHD while facilitating its integration into clinical workflows.

In light of these complexities, healthcare organizations must establish comprehensive data governance frameworks that embrace the principles of transparency, accountability, and ethical stewardship. By fostering a culture of compliance and investing in cutting-edge technologies, healthcare providers can protect patient information while harnessing the power of data to improve clinical decision-making and patient outcomes.

Approaching the significance of HIPAA with a commitment to excellence in data governance is not merely a regulatory obligation; it is a vital aspect of earning and maintaining patient trust. As health information technology continues to evolve, the alignment of data governance practices with HIPAA will be crucial in navigating the intersection of innovation and patient privacy, ultimately ensuring that healthcare organizations fulfill their mandate of providing quality care while safeguarding health information.

2.2 General Data Protection Regulation (GDPR)

The General Data Protection Regulation (GDPR) is a cornerstone of data protection legislation in the European Union, reshaping how organizations manage and process personal information, particularly in sensitive sectors such as healthcare. In a domain characterized by the vast amounts of personal data it handles, GDPR imposes rigorous requirements that compel healthcare IT systems to prioritize the privacy and security of patient information.

One of the defining features of GDPR is its focus on personal data, which includes any information that can be used to identify an individual, such as names, addresses, medical history, and even biometric data. In the context of healthcare, where data sensitivity is paramount, the regulation classifies health-related information as sensitive personal data. The stipulations of GDPR compel healthcare providers, researchers, and IT vendors to adhere to stringent guidelines to safeguard patient data throughout its lifecycle, from collection to processing and storage.

Significantly, GDPR introduces the principle of data minimization, which mandates that organizations collect only the data necessary for their stated purposes. In healthcare IT, this principle is particularly crucial, given the propensity to accumulate extensive data sets that may exceed what is essential for diagnosis, treatment, or management of patient care. This compels healthcare institutions to adopt more disciplined data governance practices, ensuring that they do not collect, retain, or process excessive or irrelevant patient information.

In addition, the regulation mandates explicit consent from individuals before their data can be processed. In the healthcare sector, obtaining informed consent can be challenging due to the complex nature of medical procedures and patient comprehension. This necessitates that healthcare organizations invest in transparent communication strategies, ensuring that consent mechanisms are clear, comprehensive, and accessible. Consequently, the integration of patient-friendly interfaces in electronic health record (EHR) systems becomes imperative, facilitating informed consent while fostering trust between patients and healthcare providers.

Another pivotal component of GDPR is the requirement for organizations to implement data protection by design and by default. This principle compels healthcare IT systems to incorporate robust security measures at the outset of system design rather than as an afterthought. For instance, when developing health applications or EHR systems, organizations must conduct Privacy Impact Assessments (PIAs) to identify potential privacy risks and integrate mitigation strategies from the onset. Such proactive measures are vital in safeguarding against data breaches, which can have devastating ramifications for both patients and organizations, leading to financial penalties, reputational damage, and loss of patient trust.

Moreover, GDPR emphasizes the importance of data protection officers (DPOs) within organizations that process significant volumes of personal data. In healthcare, DPOs play a crucial role in ensuring compliance with GDPR requirements, overseeing data management practices, conducting training programs, monitoring data processing activities, and serving as a point of contact for both patients and regulatory authorities. The DPO's appointment enables healthcare organizations to better navigate the complex landscape of data regulations and reinforces the commitment to safeguarding patient information.

Breach notification is another critical aspect of GDPR, where organizations are required to report certain types of data breaches to authorities within a 72-hour window. Non-compliance can lead to significant fines and legal repercussions. For healthcare organizations, which are attractive targets for cybercriminals due to the valuable nature of health data, establishing robust incident response protocols is essential. This includes conducting regular security audits, implementing advanced encryption practices, and fostering a culture of vigilance among staff to detect and respond to potential breaches effectively.

Accountability lies at the heart of GDPR. Organizations must maintain records of their processing activities and demonstrate compliance with the regulations. This requirement necessitates that healthcare IT systems not only monitor data access and usage but also ensure that vendors and partners comply with GDPR standards. The rise of a collaborative ecosystem in healthcare, which often involves sharing patient data among various stakeholders, highlights the importance of transparency and accountability in data governance.

Importantly, the regulation grants patients significant rights concerning their data, such as the right to access, rectify, and erase personal information held by organizations. In the context of healthcare IT, this empowers patients to take control of their health data. As patients increasingly seek autonomy in managing their health information, healthcare organizations must develop user-friendly interfaces that facilitate easy access and modification of records, thus enhancing patient engagement and satisfaction.

The international implications of GDPR extend beyond EU borders. Organizations outside of the EU that process the personal data of EU residents must also comply with GDPR, creating a ripple effect through global healthcare IT systems. This necessitates that healthcare organizations conduct thorough assessments of their data practices and policies to ensure compliance, thereby reinforcing the overarching theme of data governance in healthcare: the imperative to protect and respect patient data regardless of geographic boundaries.

In summary, GDPR imposes significant responsibilities on healthcare IT organizations that underscore the necessity of adopting robust data governance frameworks. It not only forces a reevaluation of data handling practices but also instills a culture of accountability and transparency in dealing with personal health information. As the landscape of healthcare continues to evolve with advancements in technology and data analytics, embracing the tenets of GDPR becomes indispensable in building trust and ensuring the ethical management of patient information.

2.3 Other Relevant Regulations and Standards

In the context of healthcare IT, the landscape of data governance is significantly influenced by a labyrinth of regulations and standards that aim to safeguard patient information while promoting the responsible use of data. This intricately woven fabric of frameworks serves as a foundation for maintaining data integrity, privacy, and security. A comprehensive understanding of these regulations and standards is essential for healthcare organizations striving to enhance their data governance practices.

At the forefront of data governance in healthcare is the Health Insurance Portability and Accountability Act (HIPAA) of 1996, which established critical standards for the protection of health information. While HIPAA primarily focuses on privacy and security, its implications extend into various facets of data governance, mandating that healthcare entities implement comprehensive policies and procedures. Compliance with the Privacy Rule ensures that protected health information (PHI) is accessed, used, and disclosed appropriately, pushing organizations to adopt robust data governance frameworks to monitor and enforce these regulations.

Beyond HIPAA, the Health Information Technology for Economic and Clinical Health (HITECH) Act introduced significant enhancements to the privacy and security provisions in response to the rise of electronic health records (EHRs). HITECH not only reinforced HIPAA's mandates but also emphasized the importance of Meaningful Use, which incentivizes healthcare providers to effectively adopt and use EHRs. This act catalyzed the need for healthcare organizations to establish governance structures that address the lifecycle management of health information, ensuring consistent data quality and interoperability. Compliance with HITECH necessitates meticulous reporting of breaches and the implementation of audit controls, which together form a comprehensive governance strategy.

The emergence of the 21st Century Cures Act further underscores the importance of interoperability in healthcare IT. The regulations aim to enhance the availability and utilization of electronic health information, facilitating seamless data exchange among various stakeholders. By mandating that healthcare providers and health IT developers ensure that their systems are not only interoperable but also avoid information blocking, the Cures Act promotes transparency in data governance practices. The act necessitates that organizations adopt data governance policies to address data sharing protocols, thereby fostering collaboration and improving care outcomes.

In recent years, the Federal Risk and Authorization Management Program (FEDRAMP) has gained prominence, particularly for healthcare organizations leveraging cloud computing technologies. FEDRAMP provides a standardized approach to security assessment and authorization for cloud services. Healthcare organizations must align their data governance frameworks with FEDRAMP requirements to ensure that their cloud solutions maintain the integrity and confidentiality of sensitive health data. Compliance with FEDRAMP emphasizes the need for continuous monitoring, risk assessments, and proper documentation, promoting a culture of accountability within organizations.

The National Institute of Standards and Technology (NIST) also plays a pivotal role in shaping data governance practices, providing guidance on risk management and security frameworks. The NIST Cybersecurity Framework and the Special Publication 800 series offer invaluable resources for healthcare organizations to develop and implement effective data governance strategies. By aligning with NIST standards, organizations can enhance their risk management capabilities, establish protective measures against data breaches, and foster a culture of security awareness. Adhering to NIST guidelines is essential for ensuring that data governance practices are both resilient and responsive to the evolving threat landscape.

Alongside U.S. regulations, global standards such as the General Data Protection Regulation (GDPR) have left an indelible mark on data governance approaches in healthcare. Although GDPR is a European Union regulation, its extraterritorial applicability means that any organization handling the data of EU citizens must adhere to its stringent privacy standards. GDPR mandates explicit consent for data processing, individuals' rights to access and erase their data, and strict penalties for non-compliance. Healthcare organizations operating internationally must integrate GDPR into their data governance frameworks to safeguard against potential violations and enhance patient trust.

Moreover, best practice standards, such as those proposed by the Health Information Management Systems Society (HIMSS), serve as valuable touchstones for effective data governance in healthcare. HIMSS outlines a framework that emphasizes the significance of data quality and integrity, interoperability, and risk management. By adhering to such standards, healthcare organizations can improve their data governance practices, thereby enhancing clinical outcomes and operational efficiencies. This integration of industry best practices encourages a coherent approach to data management that aligns with regulatory requirements while promoting innovation.

Additionally, the emergence of frameworks like the Data Management Association's (DAMA) Data Management Body of Knowledge (DMBOK) provides healthcare organizations with structured guidelines for comprehensive data governance. DMBOK emphasizes data stewardship, data architecture, data integration, and data quality management, all of which are fundamental to establishing a sound data governance framework. By adopting the principles laid out in DMBOK, organizations can enhance their capabilities in managing health information effectively, laying a solid foundation for decision-making and compliance.

In conclusion, the evolving regulatory landscape and standards related to data governance in healthcare IT highlight the imperative for organizations to establish robust frameworks that prioritize patient privacy, data integrity, and security. Compliance with regulations such as HIPAA, HITECH, and GDPR, alongside adherence to best practices and standards set forth by NIST and HIMSS, forms the bedrock of effective governance. As healthcare organizations navigate the complexities of data management, embracing these regulations and standards will not only bolster compliance efforts but also pave the way for innovation and improved patient outcomes.

Chapter 3: Data Privacy Principles in Healthcare

Data privacy principles in healthcare are foundational to the ethical and effective management of healthcare IT systems. As healthcare increasingly relies on digital records, the protection of patient information has become paramount. A robust framework for data privacy is critical not only for compliance with laws and regulations but also for maintaining patient trust and ensuring the integrity of healthcare delivery.

The first principle of data privacy in healthcare is the concept of confidentiality. Confidentiality refers to the obligation of healthcare providers and institutions to protect personal health information (PHI) from unauthorized access. This principle is enshrined in regulations such as the Health Insurance Portability and Accountability Act (HIPAA) in the U.S., which mandates that healthcare organizations implement safeguards to prevent breaches of patient data. To uphold confidentiality, rigorous access controls must be instituted, ensuring that only authorized personnel can access sensitive information and that data collected is used solely for intended healthcare purposes.

Another key principle is the minimization of data collection. The principle of data minimization advocates that healthcare providers should only collect information that is essential for patient care and relevant administrative functions. This not only reduces the risk of data breaches but also respects patient autonomy and privacy. By focusing on the necessity of data collection, healthcare organizations can streamline their data management practices and limit the potential fallout associated with unnecessary exposure of sensitive information.

In conjunction with minimization, the principle of data accuracy plays a crucial role in healthcare data privacy. Accurate data is fundamental for effective treatment and clinical decision-making. Errors in patient information can lead to misdiagnoses and inappropriate treatment, compromising patient welfare. Healthcare providers must adopt stringent data validation processes to ensure that the information collected is current, complete, and correct. Implementing regular audits and updates of patient records can significantly enhance data accuracy, thereby building a more reliable healthcare ecosystem.

The transparency principle also governs healthcare data privacy, requiring organizations to openly communicate their data practices to patients. Patients have a right to know how their information is collected, used, and shared. This transparency fosters trust and empowers patients to engage actively in their own care. Clear privacy policies and consent forms are vital in elucidating patient rights and the extent of data usage. Patients should be informed about their options regarding data sharing and be able to opt-in or opt-out as per their comfort levels.

Security is another fundamental principle within the realm of data privacy. This principle encompasses the protective measures that safeguard PHI against unauthorized access, theft, and loss. Healthcare organizations are tasked with employing state-of-the-art security protocols, including encryption, firewalls, and intrusion detection systems. Furthermore, conducting regular risk assessments and training staff on security best practices is essential to cultivate a culture of awareness and responsiveness to potential threats.

Moreover, the principle of accountability emphasizes that healthcare organizations must establish clear governance structures to ensure compliance with data privacy regulations. Accountability mechanisms involve assigning responsibility for data governance to specific individuals or departments, thereby facilitating oversight and adherence to policies. Furthermore, organizations should foster an ethos of accountability by regularly reviewing their privacy practices and implementing corrective actions as needed. This proactive stance not only enhances compliance with regulations but also mitigates risks associated with data breaches.

Data retention policies contribute significantly to privacy principles by defining how long patient data should be kept. Effective data governance mandates that healthcare organizations establish clear guidelines for data retention and disposal. Retaining data longer than necessary increases exposure risks and complicates compliance with regulations such as HIPAA. On the other hand, a rigid approach to data destruction may lead to the unintended loss of critical clinical information. Thus, a balanced approach that aligns data retention practices with clinical needs and regulatory requirements is essential.

Upon the advent of emerging technologies such as artificial intelligence and machine learning in healthcare, the principle of informed consent has gained renewed importance. Patients must be made aware of how these technologies might utilize their data and the implications for their privacy. It is imperative for healthcare organizations to obtain explicit consent from patients before using their data in research or analytics. This not only aligns with ethical standards but also reinforces trust in technology-driven healthcare solutions.

Lastly, the principle of ongoing evaluation and adaptation acknowledges that as technology evolves, so too must data privacy practices. Continuous monitoring and assessment of data privacy measures ensure that policies remain effective amidst emerging threats and changing regulatory landscapes. Regular training, updates, and audits can aid in identifying weaknesses in current practices and facilitate opportunities for enhancement.

In conclusion, a commitment to data privacy principles is indispensable in healthcare IT governance. Emphasizing confidentiality, minimization, accuracy, transparency, security, accountability, data retention, informed consent, and ongoing evaluation forms the bedrock of a trustworthy healthcare environment. As these principles are harmoniously integrated into healthcare practices, patient rights are safeguarded, and the potential for innovation within the healthcare sector can be fully realized, ultimately leading to improved outcomes and enhanced patient care.

3.1 Patient Consent and Autonomy

In the rapidly evolving landscape of healthcare IT, the principles of patient consent and autonomy play a critical role in shaping the framework through which data governance is executed. At the intersection of technological advancement and ethical responsibility lies the imperative to prioritize the rights of patients as data subjects. Central to this is the understanding that data governance mechanisms must not only comply with legal standards but also foster an environment where patient autonomy is respected and reinforced.

Patient consent is not merely a bureaucratic formality; it is the bedrock of ethical medical practice. The advent of electronic health records (EHR), mobile health applications, and predictive analytics has compounded the complexity surrounding data collection and utilization in healthcare. Consequently, the notion of informed consent has undergone significant transformation. In a traditional setting, informed consent was often illustrated through a one-time interaction, wherein patients were provided with printed materials detailing the risks and benefits associated with a treatment. However, as healthcare increasingly integrates digital modalities, it becomes imperative to evolve the definition of informed consent to encompass ongoing data use and sharing practices.

To operationalize informed consent in a digitized environment, healthcare organizations must develop frameworks that enable dynamic consent processes. This approach empowers patients to make granular decisions about their data, effectively allowing them to give or withdraw consent at various stages. Dynamic consent not only enhances the patient's ability to control their information but also fosters trust, a cornerstone of the provider-patient relationship. Engaging patients through user-friendly interfaces and transparent communication can significantly impact their understanding of what their consent entails, especially regarding secondary uses of their data for research or commercial purposes.

Autonomy extends beyond the mere act of consenting; it encapsulates the patient's right to make choices concerning their health. In the context of data governance, this autonomy is often challenged by the very technologies designed to improve care delivery. Automated decision-making tools, predictive analytics, and machine learning algorithms can, at times, obscure the decision pathways and inadvertently undermine patient agency. It becomes vital, therefore, to ensure that autonomy is not just preserved but actively promoted through robust governance frameworks.

Healthcare IT stakeholders must consider the implications of their data practices on patient autonomy. For instance, algorithmic transparency is essential for enabling patients to understand how their data may influence decision-making processes. By fostering an environment where patients can access understandable explanations of how algorithms function and the reasoning behind care recommendations, practitioners enhance patients' capacity to make informed choices about their health.

Moreover, robust data governance frameworks must address the risks associated with data misuse and breaches. The unauthorized access to or sharing of personal health information can have profound consequences, impacting patient trust and willingness to consent to future data use. Establishing strict data stewardship protocols, such as data anonymization techniques and stringent access controls, can mitigate these risks and safeguard patient autonomy.

Legal and ethical frameworks also play a pivotal role in governing patient consent and autonomy. Regulations such as the Health Insurance Portability and Accountability Act (HIPAA) in the United States and the General Data Protection Regulation (GDPR) in the European Union provide foundational guidelines concerning patient data rights. These regulations highlight not only the necessity for explicit consent but also the right of patients to access, amend, and delete their data. Understanding these legal instruments is critical for healthcare providers and IT stakeholders who are tasked with implementing data governance policies that align with both ethical principles and compliance obligations.

Furthermore, the evolution of the relationship between patients and healthcare providers necessitates a rethinking of consent models. Traditionally, patients were passive recipients of care, often deferring to the authority of medical professionals. However, contemporary patients seek to be engaged and informed partners in their own healthcare journey. This shift calls for healthcare organizations to adopt participatory approaches to data governance, whereby patients are actively involved in discussions concerning their data and its use. Such collaboration can take many forms, from focus groups to public forums, allowing patients to voice their preferences and concerns directly.

Training and education for healthcare providers in the nuances of patient consent and autonomy are also indispensable. Enhanced awareness of the ethical implications of data handling can prepare providers to navigate complex discussions with patients regarding their data rights. Equipping healthcare professionals with effective communication strategies enables them to articulate the value of consent while addressing potential concerns around data privacy and security.

In conclusion, patient consent and autonomy are essential pillars within the realm of data governance in healthcare IT.

The integration of robust, dynamic consent processes, the maintenance of algorithmic transparency, the application of stringent data protection measures, and the promotion of participatory approaches must all be prioritized. As healthcare continues to embrace innovative technologies, the emphasis on patient rights will not only ensure ethical compliance but will also cultivate a supportive environment in which patients feel empowered, valued, and engaged in their own healthcare decisions. It is through this commitment to patient-centric governance that the future of healthcare IT can both thrive and adhere to the ethical imperatives that underpin the practice.

3.2 Data Minimization and Purpose Limitation

The principles of data minimization and purpose limitation are integral to effective data governance in healthcare IT, directly impacting how healthcare organizations manage patient information while adhering to legal and ethical obligations. These concepts not only promote efficient data handling practices but also support the foundational goal of protecting patient privacy and ensuring the results of healthcare IT continue to benefit all stakeholders.

Data minimization, which emanates from regulations such as the GDPR (General Data Protection Regulation), emphasizes the need to limit the collection of personal data to what is essential for the specified purpose. In healthcare, where data can include sensitive information about an individual's medical history, treatment plans, and personal identifiers, the implications of extensive data collection are manifold. Firstly, collecting only the necessary data reduces the burden of compliance with data protection regulations. It minimizes the risks associated with data breaches, as fewer records in circulation result in a diminished potential for exposure.

Moreover, data minimization fosters trust among patients. When healthcare providers articulate a clear commitment to safeguarding their patients' data by resisting the unnecessary collection and storage of personal information, it reinforces the philosophy of "do no harm." This trust is critical, as it encourages patients to share sensitive health information, which can ultimately lead to better health outcomes through accurate diagnosis and tailored treatment plans.

Additionally, data minimization correlates with operational efficiency. In healthcare environments often overwhelmed by vast amounts of data, focusing on essential information streamlines processes like data analysis and retrieval. This focus allows healthcare institutions to concentrate their resources on actionable insights derived from high-value data. Such operational efficiency paves the way for enhanced patient care, as medical professionals are empowered with relevant information without the noise created by irrelevant data.

Purpose limitation is equally important in governing healthcare data. This principle stipulates that data should be collected for specified, legitimate purposes and not be processed in ways incompatible with those initial purposes. In the context of healthcare, this means that information should only be utilized for its intended purpose, such as treatment, billing, or quality improvement initiatives.

The improper application of data can lead to significant ethical dilemmas and potentially harmful consequences for patients. For instance, using health records for unauthorized research or marketing purposes can breach patient confidentiality, eroding trust between individuals and healthcare providers. This underlines the need for transparency in how data is utilized. Patients deserve to know precisely what their information will be used for and to experience a sense of comfort that their sensitive data will not be exploited for unexpected, high-risk purposes.

Furthermore, purpose limitation aids in fostering information governance that aligns with the evolving landscape of healthcare requirements. As technology and medical practices evolve, so do the potential purposes for which data might be applied. Hence, organizations must implement robust data governance frameworks to periodically reassess and clearly communicate the purpose behind data collection and usage. This requires not only the governance of existing datasets but also meticulous planning before new data processing activities are undertaken.

The intersection of data minimization and purpose limitation presents a holistic approach to data governance in healthcare IT. When healthcare organizations adopt these principles, they create an ecosystem rooted in data ethics, compliance, and accountability. By focusing on essential data concerning established purposes, institutions can reduce the potential for misuse and enhance their operational relevance. It fosters a culture of respect for patient autonomy, aligning with the core tenets of medical ethics.

Implementing a robust framework around these principles necessitates a multidisciplinary approach. Stakeholders— ranging from IT professionals and data privacy officers to healthcare providers and legal experts—must collaborate to frame policies that champion both ethical data handling and efficient resource allocation. Adequate training and ongoing education regarding data governance policies are essential, empowering staff to navigate complexities associated with data handling while reinforcing a culture centered on privacy by design.

Yet, challenges remain in executing these principles operationally. Balancing the gaps between innovation in healthcare technologies and the imperative of strict data governance practices can present hurdles. For example, while analytics offer integral insights into patient care and operational improvements, overreliance on vast datasets without regard for these governing principles may inadvertently lead healthcare providers to misuse sensitive information.

Visualizing the future of data governance in healthcare, innovation must occur within the parameters of these core concepts. The implementation of advanced analytics, artificial intelligence, and machine learning should proceed with careful scrutiny of the ethical implications tied to the collection, analysis, and usage of patient data. Only by committing to data minimization and purpose limitation can the healthcare sector derive the maximum benefit from innovative technologies while upholding a steadfast commitment to safeguarding patient rights.

In sum, the strategies underpinning data minimization and purpose limitation are crucial to shaping a responsible and ethical data governance framework within healthcare IT. These principles advance not only legal compliance but also foster patient trust, operational efficiency, and data integrity, which are paramount in an era where the digital landscape is becoming increasingly complex. Embracing these guiding principles equips healthcare organizations to navigate the challenges posed by rapid technological advancement while truly prioritizing their core mission: patient care.

3.3 Data Security Measures

In the realm of healthcare IT, ensuring data security is paramount due to the sensitive nature of personal health information (PHI) and the increasingly stringent regulatory requirements. Effective data security measures serve as the backbone of data governance, ensuring compliance, protecting patient privacy, and maintaining the integrity of healthcare systems. These measures hinge upon a multifaceted approach that combines technological solutions, policy frameworks, and a well-informed workforce.

First and foremost, establishing a robust access control framework is essential for protecting data. Role-Based Access Control (RBAC) and Attribute-Based Access Control (ABAC) mechanisms form the basis of this approach, whereby access to sensitive data is granted based on the specific role of the user or attributes related to the user. This ensures that only authorized personnel, such as healthcare providers and administrative staff, have access to PHI. Additionally, implementing the principle of least privilege further limits access to only the data necessary for an individual's role. This minimized access reduces the risk of internal breaches, whether accidental or malicious.

Encryption plays a critical role in safeguarding data both at rest and in transit. In healthcare, data is often transmitted between various entities, such as providers, insurance companies, and patients. High-level encryption algorithms protect data integrity by making information unintelligible to unauthorized users. Advanced Encryption Standard (AES) is a widely recognized encryption standard that has been adopted for securing sensitive healthcare data. Furthermore, securing data at rest using full-disk encryption helps protect data stored on servers and devices, ensuring that even if a device is compromised, the data remains protected. Regular audits of encryption methods and updates to protocols are necessary steps to stay ahead of potential vulnerabilities.

Regularly conducted risk assessments form an integral part of any data security strategy. These assessments allow healthcare organizations to identify potential threats and vulnerabilities within their systems. By employing risk assessment methodologies such as NIST Special Publication 800-30, organizations can create a comprehensive understanding of their security posture. Furthermore, these assessments should not be one-time events; instead, they should be integrated into a continuous improvement framework. As technology and cyber threats evolve, so should the assessment techniques and the corresponding security measures.

Data backups represent another crucial security measure. By implementing a robust data backup strategy, healthcare organizations can mitigate the risk of data loss due to ransomware attacks, system failures, or accidental deletions. Regularly scheduled, encrypted backups stored offsite provide a safety net, ensuring that data can be restored with minimal disruption to operations and continuity of care. It's vital that organizations also test their data restoration processes to verify that backups are reliable and can be restored promptly when needed.

Implementing strong network security measures is fundamental to thwarting unauthorized access to sensitive data. Firewalls, intrusion detection systems (IDS), and intrusion prevention systems (IPS) act as first lines of defense against external attacks. A layered security approach, known as defense-in-depth, combines these technologies to create multiple barriers, deterring cybercriminals. Thus, even if attackers penetrate one layer, subsequent layers still provide protection. Additionally, establishing a Virtual Private Network (VPN) for remote access can offer an additional layer of security by encrypting connections, thereby safeguarding sensitive data during transmission.

User training and awareness are often overlooked yet critical aspects of data security. Human error is frequently cited as a leading cause of data breaches in healthcare settings. Comprehensive training programs should be instituted to educate employees about data protection protocols, phishing attacks, and the importance of safeguarding patient information. Regularly scheduled refresher courses and simulated phishing exercises can reinforce security awareness and foster a culture of vigilance within the organization.

Integrating security controls into the software development lifecycle (SDLC) is also imperative. As healthcare organizations increasingly adopt electronic health records (EHRs) and other applications, ensuring that these systems are developed with security in mind is vital to minimizing vulnerabilities. Using frameworks like the Secure Development Lifecycle (SDL) enables organizations to mitigate risks by addressing security concerns from the early stages of system development to deployment and maintenance.

Compliance with regulatory standards is fundamental to data security in healthcare. Regulations such as the Health Insurance Portability and Accountability Act (HIPAA) set specific standards for safeguarding PHI. Compliance not only fosters trust among patients and stakeholders but also reinforces data security measures. Regular compliance audits, not as mere checkboxes but as opportunities to identify areas for improvement, are necessary to ensure ongoing adherence to regulatory requirements.

Finally, incident response planning is a vital component of data security measures. Despite the most stringent precautions, breaches can still occur. Having an incident response plan in place enables organizations to act swiftly to mitigate damage, report incidents to regulatory authorities, and communicate effectively with affected parties. Continuous refinement of the response plan based on lessons learned from past incidents enhances an organization's resilience to future threats.

In summary, adopting a comprehensive approach to data security is integral to effective data governance in healthcare IT. By addressing access controls, employing encryption, conducting regular risk assessments, ensuring reliable data backups, and fostering a culture of awareness among employees, healthcare organizations can significantly bolster their defenses against data breaches. Compliance adherence, along with incident response planning, completes the robust framework necessary for protecting the integrity, confidentiality, and availability of sensitive healthcare data.

Chapter 4: Data Quality Management in Healthcare IT

In the realm of healthcare IT, data quality management emerges as a crucial pillar supporting the edifice of effective data governance. As healthcare institutions increasingly rely on data analytics for patient care, operational efficiency, and strategic planning, the quality of data becomes paramount. Ensuring accuracy, completeness, consistency, and timeliness is not merely a technical requirement; it is a critical enabler of healthcare quality, safety, and efficiency.

The merging of healthcare services and technology has created an environment where vast amounts of data are generated, collected, and analyzed. This data spans electronic health records (EHRs), billing databases, patient management systems, and clinical decision support systems. However, despite the technological advancements, healthcare organizations often grapple with data discrepancies that can compromise patient outcomes and operational performance. Thus, implementing robust data quality management practices within the framework of data governance is essential.

Data quality management is multifaceted and encompasses several core dimensions. Accuracy refers to how closely data represents real-world conditions; completeness relates to the extent to which all required data is collected; consistency involves the uniformity of data across different systems; and timeliness encompasses the data's availability when needed. In healthcare, these dimensions can deeply influence clinical decisions, medical billing, compliance with regulations, and research outcomes. Poor data quality can lead to misdiagnosis, inappropriate treatment plans, and even adverse patient events, highlighting why healthcare organizations must prioritize data integrity.

The governance model employed by a healthcare organization should integrate a structured approach to data quality management. Establishing a framework that delineates roles and responsibilities for data stewardship is critical. Data stewards are responsible for ensuring the adherence to data quality standards. Their duties include monitoring data inputs, addressing errors, and conducting regular audits to assess data quality levels. Prominent roles such as Chief Data Officer (CDO) or Chief Information Officer (CIO) often oversee these efforts, creating an authoritative presence that emphasizes the importance of data quality across the organization.

Moreover, the establishment of data quality metrics is fundamental. Organizations should identify specific, measurable indicators that reflect the health of their data. Metrics could include the rate of data entry errors, the percentage of missing values, and the frequency of data updates. These evaluations are not merely isolated reports but should be integrated into organizational performance dashboards, facilitating a continuous feedback loop that informs decision-making processes. Harnessing advanced technologies such as artificial intelligence and machine learning can also refine data quality assessment, enabling proactive identification of anomalies before they escalate.

Training and education are crucial components in nurturing a culture of data quality awareness within healthcare organizations. Stakeholders across all levels, from clinicians to administrative staff, must understand the implications of data quality and their role in maintaining it. Regular workshops, seminars, and the integration of data quality principles in onboarding programs can cultivate a workforce that prioritizes precise and accurate data entry, promoting a holistic approach to data governance.

The establishment of standardized data governance policies and frameworks is imperative for balancing the disparate systems that often characterize healthcare IT environments.

The adoption of standards such as Health Level Seven International (HL7) and Fast Healthcare Interoperability Resources (FHIR) promotes interoperability and data exchange across systems. Organizations must standardize data definitions, formats, and terminologies to minimize inconsistency and improve communication across various stakeholders, including patients, providers, regulators, and insurers.

Compliance with regulatory frameworks, such as the Health Insurance Portability and Accountability Act (HIPAA) and the Centers for Medicare & Medicaid Services (CMS) guidelines, further underscores the necessity of data quality management. Ensuring that data adheres to regulatory requirements not only enhances data integrity but also minimizes the risk of legal ramifications that can arise from data breaches or inaccuracies. Consequently, comprehensive training in data governance is vital for compliance officers and organizational leaders who must navigate the intricate landscape of healthcare regulations.

Integrating patient engagement strategies can also positively impact data quality. Encouraging patients to provide accurate and complete information during their interactions with the healthcare system creates a partnership in data stewardship. Implementing user-friendly interfaces for patient input, such as online portals or mobile applications, can facilitate better data collection and reduce human error. Additionally, patients who actively participate in managing their health records can become advocates for data quality improvements, ensuring their healthcare narratives are accurately reflected in the data that supports their care.

In conclusion, effective data quality management is indispensable in the context of healthcare IT governance. As the healthcare landscape continues to evolve with new technologies and increasing data volumes, organizations must adopt comprehensive strategies that ensure data quality underpins every facet of care delivery. Through a combination of robust frameworks, proactive training, adherence to standardized practices, and patient engagement, healthcare organizations can safeguard the integrity of their data. Ultimately, this proactive approach to data quality not only enhances operational efficiency but also drives improvements in patient outcomes, thereby fulfilling the overarching mission of healthcare: to provide safe, effective, and patient-centered care.

4.1 Importance of Data Accuracy and Completeness

Data accuracy and completeness are critical components of data governance in healthcare IT, with profound implications for patient safety, regulatory compliance, and operational efficiency. In an era where healthcare systems increasingly rely on digital data repositories for decision-making, the accuracy and completeness of this data must be prioritized to ensure optimal outcomes. Flawed data can lead to misguided clinical decisions, financial repercussions, and regulatory scrutiny, highlighting the importance of robust data governance frameworks.

First and foremost, accurate data is paramount in clinical decision-making. Healthcare providers need reliable information to make informed decisions regarding diagnoses, treatment plans, and patient management. Inaccurate data can lead to adverse outcomes, such as misdiagnoses, inappropriate treatments, and even fatalities. For example, a healthcare provider who mistakenly interprets incomplete medication history due to data inaccuracies may prescribe incompatible drugs, risking patient well-being. As such, health information systems must prioritize data integrity, employing stringent validation protocols and real-time data quality assessments to ensure that the information feeds into clinical workflows is both accurate and comprehensive.

Beyond patient safety, data accuracy and completeness play a crucial role in operational efficiency. Healthcare organizations operate in an environment characterized by complex workflows, regulatory requirements, and financial constraints. With the pressures to deliver quality care while managing costs, healthcare organizations must rely on accurate data analytics to streamline operations, optimize resource allocation, and enhance revenue cycles. For instance, billing systems depend heavily on precise patient data; discrepancies can lead to denied claims, prolonging revenue collection periods and straining financial resources. In this context, comprehensive data governance that encompasses meticulous data management practices is essential to minimize errors and ensure operational effectiveness.

Moreover, regulatory compliance mandates a stringent focus on data accuracy and completeness. Health organizations are bound by numerous regulations, such as the Health Insurance Portability and Accountability Act (HIPAA) and the Centers for Medicare & Medicaid Services (CMS) guidelines, which require secure, accurate documentation of patient data. Non-compliance can result in severe penalties, including fines and loss of accreditation. Therefore, adherence to a robust data governance framework that emphasizes quality and completeness not only mitigates risks but also enhances the credibility of healthcare institutions. Engaging stakeholders—ranging from clinical staff to data analysts—in the data governance process contributes to a culture that prioritizes data quality, ensuring ongoing compliance with evolving regulations.

In addition to clinical and operational considerations, healthcare data accuracy influences population health management and research initiatives. In the era of value-based care, healthcare organizations are increasingly held accountable for population health outcomes. To implement effective interventions, organizations must analyze large datasets to understand trends, identify at-risk populations, and evaluate the efficacy of healthcare delivery models. Inaccurate or incomplete data can skew these analyses, yielding unreliable conclusions that could misguide public health initiatives. For research purposes, data integrity is equally crucial; inaccurate data compromises the validity of clinical studies, ultimately undermining evidence-based practices. Consequently, a commitment to data accuracy and completeness is fundamental not only for immediate patient care but also for advancing public health and healthcare research.

Implementing data governance frameworks that emphasize accuracy and completeness illustrates the multifaceted nature of these concepts. Key components include data stewardship, data quality management, and robust training programs. Data stewardship involves assigning responsibilities for data quality across the organization, ensuring that designated personnel monitor data entry processes and manage anomalies. This practice empowers clinical and administrative staff to take ownership of data as a critical asset, fostering a sense of accountability.

Data quality management encompasses continuous monitoring and auditing of data quality metrics, facilitating the identification of gaps and inaccuracies. Organizations may leverage advanced technologies, such as artificial intelligence and machine learning, to automate data quality assessments and mitigate human error. Continuous improvement processes ensure that organizations adapt to changing data environments while maintaining high-quality standards.

Training programs tailored to the unique needs of healthcare professionals also play an instrumental role in promoting data accuracy and completeness. Education initiatives should focus on the significance of accurate data entry, the impact of missing information, and compliance with established data governance policies. By cultivating a culture of data literacy, organizations empower their workforce to recognize the importance of data integrity in daily operations and patient interactions.

Finally, achieving data accuracy and completeness requires collaboration across various stakeholders within healthcare ecosystems. This includes engaging IT professionals, clinical staff, and administrative personnel in conversations about data governance, fostering a shared vision for data quality improvement. Implementing feedback loops allows for continuous evaluation and enhancement of data practices, ensuring that the organization remains agile amidst the complexities of healthcare data management.

In conclusion, the emphasis on data accuracy and completeness within healthcare IT cannot be overstated. These elements are integral not only for enhancing patient safety and operational efficiency but also for ensuring regulatory compliance and advancing population health initiatives. Organizations that prioritize robust data governance frameworks are better positioned to harness the power of data as a vital asset in their pursuit of high-quality healthcare delivery. By fostering a culture of accountability and leveraging technology, healthcare entities can pave the way for improved outcomes and transformative innovations in the rapidly evolving landscape of the industry.

4.2 Techniques for Maintaining Data Quality

Data quality is integral to effective healthcare IT systems, influencing clinical decisions, regulatory compliance, and operational efficiency. To ensure that the data driving these systems remains accurate, complete, and consistent, various techniques can be employed. These techniques not only encompass data capture and storage but also emphasize ongoing data management practices. Recognizing and implementing these methodologies is paramount for organizations aiming to achieve robust data governance in the healthcare domain.

One fundamental technique is data validation, which involves verifying the accuracy and integrity of data at the point of entry. Implementing validation checks during data input processes can prevent many inaccuracies from entering systems. For instance, when patient demographics are recorded, real-time validation can ensure formats meet specific standards and that required fields are filled. Electronic health record (EHR) systems can utilize automated rules that flag discrepancies or incomplete entries, prompting users to correct errors before finalizing input. Such proactive measures diminish the downstream effects of poor-quality data, safeguarding the reliability of patient records.

Data cleansing is another essential technique, focusing on identifying and rectifying errors in datasets. Over time, databases can become cluttered with duplicates, outdated information, or erroneous entries. Regularly scheduled data cleaning processes can streamline the data landscape, enhancing the quality and usability of information stored within a health IT system. Data cleansing not only improves operational efficiency but also strengthens decision-making.

For example, if a database contains multiple entries for the same patient, it may lead to confusion over medical histories, impacting care delivery. Thus, routine audits and the establishment of protocols for data cleansing are crucial components of a comprehensive data governance strategy.

Another vital technique is the implementation of data standards. Standardization across systems allows for the uniformity of data formats and terminologies, which is particularly important in healthcare given the myriad of diverse systems in use. The adoption of industry-specific standards, such as HL7 and SNOMED, fosters interoperability among systems, ensuring that data can be effectively shared and utilized across different platforms. Moreover, standardization facilitates more efficient data aggregation and analysis, making it easier for healthcare organizations to derive insights from their data.

Metadata management also plays a critical role in maintaining data quality. Metadata provides context to the data being used, defining attributes such as source, format, and relevance. Effective metadata management ensures that users can understand the origin and usability of data, which is essential for informed decision-making. By establishing a robust framework for metadata, healthcare organizations can improve the discoverability and reliability of data assets. This clarity can significantly enhance data quality by ensuring that users have access to the most accurate and relevant information when needed.

Training and education of staff are pivotal in promoting a culture of data quality within healthcare organizations. Employees must be knowledgeable about the importance of accurate data entry and the implications of poor-quality data on clinical outcomes. Ongoing training sessions, workshops, and the dissemination of best practices can empower staff to contribute actively to data governance efforts. Additionally, fostering an organizational culture that prioritizes data integrity helps create accountability among team members, reinforcing the significance of their role in maintaining data quality.

Another effective approach is the establishment of a data stewardship program. Appointing data stewards—individuals responsible for managing data quality, integrity, and usage—can provide a focused effort toward maintaining high data standards. These stewards serve as advocates for data governance, ensuring adherence to policies and procedures pertaining to data collection and management. They can conduct regular assessments of data quality and provide valuable insights into areas needing improvement. The presence of dedicated personnel allows organizations to take a more systematic approach to data quality, aligning data governance initiatives with broader organizational goals.

Data monitoring and analytics can further enhance data quality over time. Establishing metrics for data quality helps organizations quantify performance and identify trends in data discrepancies. Anomalies can be detected through automated monitoring systems that flag unusual patterns or deviations from expected data norms. This proactive approach enables organizations to respond quickly to potential data issues before they escalate into larger problems. By leveraging analytical tools, healthcare organizations can derive actionable insights from their data, informing decisions that facilitate continuous improvements in data quality.

Collaboration across departments is also crucial in maintaining data quality. Healthcare is inherently interdisciplinary, with various stakeholders—administrators, clinicians, IT professionals—engaged in data generation and usage. Establishing collaborative frameworks encourages communication among these groups, allowing them to share best practices and insights that enhance data quality. Cross-departmental meetings and feedback loops can facilitate transparency and ensure that issues are addressed collectively.

Lastly, leveraging technology such as artificial intelligence (AI) and machine learning (ML) can play a transformative role in maintaining data quality. These advanced technologies can automate routine data quality checks, assist in data cleansing, and predict potential quality issues based on historical data trends. AI and ML-driven algorithms can identify patterns and anomalies that human oversight may miss, thus enabling more effective data governance.

In conclusion, maintaining data quality within healthcare IT requires a multifaceted approach that encompasses validation, cleansing, standardization, and monitoring, complemented by staff education and interdisciplinary collaboration. By employing these techniques, healthcare organizations can cultivate a culture of data integrity, ultimately enhancing clinical outcomes and operational efficiency. Prioritizing data quality is not merely a technical necessity but a foundational element of effective healthcare governance.

4.3 Data Quality Metrics and Assessment

Data quality is an essential component of effective healthcare IT systems, influencing patient safety, clinical outcomes, and operational efficiency. In the context of data governance, establishing robust data quality metrics and assessment methods becomes paramount. These metrics serve as benchmarks for evaluating the accuracy, completeness, consistency, timeliness, and relevance of healthcare data. By systematically assessing these dimensions, healthcare organizations can identify deficiencies and implement improvements, ultimately enhancing the quality of care provided to patients.

Accuracy is a fundamental metric in data quality assessment, reflecting how closely data values align with their true values. In healthcare, accurate data are essential for clinical decision-making, billing, and reporting purposes. For example, inaccurate patient demographics can lead to misdiagnosis or inappropriate treatment plans. Metrics such as the proportion of data entries free of error or the validation rate against external sources are instrumental in measuring accuracy. Implementing routine auditing processes and employing data validation techniques, such as cross-referencing with electronic health records (EHRs) and claims databases, can effectively enhance the accuracy of data collected.

Completeness assesses the extent to which expected data attributes are present in a dataset. Inadequate data capture can impede healthcare quality initiatives and analytics, leading to skewed outcomes and ineffective interventions. For instance, missing clinical data elements, such as lab results or medication histories, can hinder a clinician's comprehensive view of a patient's health status. Measuring completeness involves calculating the percentage of required fields populated in a dataset, as well as analyzing the impact of missing data on treatment decisions. Techniques such as data imputation, where missing values are estimated based on existing data, or enhancing data collection protocols can mitigate issues surrounding completeness.

Consistency, another critical metric, reflects the uniformity of data across different datasets or systems. In healthcare environments, where multiple systems generate and utilize data, inconsistencies can arise in terminologies, formats, or classifications. For example, a patient's allergy information stored in different systems might conflict, leading to potential adverse drug reactions. To assess consistency, health IT leaders can use data profiling tools that evaluate data attributes across systems, identify discrepancies, and standardize data formats where applicable. Establishing data standards and governance policies is crucial for fostering consistency, ensuring that all systems adhere to predefined protocols.

Timeliness pertains to the degree to which data is up-to-date and available for use when needed. Delayed access to critical patient information can compromise clinical decision-making and care coordination. For instance, timely updates to EHRs following lab tests are vital for productive clinical consultations. Metrics for assessing timeliness often involve tracking the latency between data collection and entry into systems, as well as the frequency of data updates. Health organizations can improve timeliness by automating data entry processes and employing real-time data integration techniques, thereby ensuring that clinicians have the most current information at their disposal.

Relevance, the final dimension to be considered, evaluates whether the data being collected serves the intended purpose and is useful for clinical and operational needs. Healthcare organizations must continuously assess whether the data elements being collected align with business objectives and regulatory requirements. This can be particularly challenging in an era of rapid technological advancements and evolving practices. Substantial metrics for relevance include the frequency with which data is accessed and utilized in decision-making processes, as well as feedback from end users on data usefulness. Conducting regular stakeholder assessments will help ensure the data being collected remains pertinent and applicable to the organization's goals.

The interplay between these data quality metrics influences overall data governance initiatives in healthcare IT. Effective data governance frameworks not only delineate the roles and responsibilities of data stewards but also establish the necessary processes for data quality management. Regular monitoring of these metrics is essential in creating a data-driven culture within healthcare organizations, where decision-makers prioritize high-quality data in navigating complex patient care landscapes.

Ultimately, a comprehensive approach to data quality metrics and assessment can foster significant improvements in healthcare delivery. By leveraging accurate, complete, consistent, timely, and relevant data, decision-makers can enhance clinical workflows, improve patient safety, and derive actionable insights for population health management. As healthcare continues to evolve, so too must the strategies for data governance, ensuring that organizations are equipped to effectively assess and uphold the integrity of their data assets.

In conclusion, the establishment of data quality metrics is not merely a technical endeavor; it is foundational to reliable and effective healthcare IT systems. As healthcare data proliferates in scope and complexity, an uncompromising focus on data quality assessment will ensure that healthcare organizations harness the full potential of their data assets to improve care, achieve operational excellence, and inspire stakeholder confidence.

Chapter 5: Roles and Responsibilities in Data Governance

Data governance in healthcare IT is a critical framework that ensures the effective management of data assets, compliance with regulations, and the overall enhancement of data quality and accessibility. As healthcare organizations increasingly rely on vast amounts of data to inform patient care, operational decisions, and research initiatives, the roles and responsibilities associated with data governance become paramount. This framework encompasses various stakeholders, each with distinct duties that contribute to the overarching goal of maintaining high standards in data management while promoting transparency and accountability.

At the helm of data governance is the Chief Data Officer (CDO) or equivalent executive leadership role. The CDO plays a pivotal role in establishing a strategic vision for data management, ensuring alignment with organizational objectives. This leadership position is responsible for fostering a data-driven culture across all levels of the organization, advocating for the integration of data governance practices into the core operations of healthcare IT. The CDO's involvement in policy creation, resource allocation, and oversight of the data governance framework is essential for enabling other stakeholders to operate effectively within this ecosystem.

The role of the data governance committee is equally significant, acting as a governing body to oversee policies and procedures related to data usage, quality, and security. Comprised of representatives from various departments—

such as IT, compliance, legal, clinical, and finance—the committee ensures that a diverse range of perspectives and expertise informs decisions. Their responsibilities include setting data governance goals, monitoring adherence to established policies, and resolving conflicting priorities or issues that may arise among stakeholders. This collaborative approach fosters a culture of shared responsibility and stakeholder engagement, critical in a multifaceted healthcare environment.

Data stewards are another integral component of the data governance framework. Tasked with the operational management of data assets, data stewards serve as the bridge between data governance policies and day-to-day data management practices. These individuals are responsible for implementing data quality protocols, classification, and validation processes, ensuring that the data used across the organization is accurate, consistent, and trustworthy. By functioning as the guardians of data integrity, data stewards also facilitate training and support for end-users, thereby promoting best practices in data handling throughout the organization.

In addition to these roles, compliance officers also play an essential function in maintaining the integrity of data governance in healthcare. Their responsibilities include ensuring adherence to regulatory requirements, such as HIPAA and GDPR, which dictate how patient data should be managed and protected. Compliance officers must remain vigilant, continuously monitoring both internal practices and external changes in legislation, to mitigate risks associated with non-compliance. This proactive approach not only safeguards the organization but also builds trust with patients and stakeholders, affirming the organization's commitment to ethical data practices.

The collaboration between data governance leaders — including the CDO, governance committee, data stewards, and compliance officers — is critical in establishing clear guidelines and processes for data management. This collaboration must extend throughout the organization, involving clinical staff, researchers, data analysts, and IT professionals. Each of these roles contributes to a comprehensive understanding of the data lifecycle, ensuring that data is properly collected, stored, processed, and utilized in a manner that aligns with organizational objectives and regulatory standards.

The engagement of clinical staff is particularly vital to data governance in healthcare. Frontline healthcare providers, such as physicians and nurses, are directly involved in data generation and use. Their insights are invaluable for understanding the context in which clinical data is collected and how it should be used to enhance patient care and outcomes. By actively involving these professionals in data governance discussions and decisions, organizations can ensure that data policies are practical and grounded in the realities of clinical practice.

Data analysts and IT professionals also hold key responsibilities related to data governance. Analysts utilize data to generate insights that drive decision-making, while IT ensures that technical infrastructures support data governance initiatives effectively. Collaborating closely with data stewards and governance committees, these professionals ensure that data quality is maintained throughout its lifecycle and that proper security measures are in place to protect sensitive information from unauthorized access or breaches. Their technical expertise, combined with an understanding of governance principles, contributes to a robust data management framework.

Training and communication represent the backbone of successful data governance in healthcare. All stakeholders must be well-informed about their roles, responsibilities, and the importance of data governance practices. Regular training sessions, workshops, and open forums for discussion can help cultivate a culture of accountability and comprehensive understanding across the organization. Frequent communication reinforces the importance of data governance, bridging gaps between diverse roles and ensuring that everyone is working collaboratively toward common objectives.

In conclusion, clearly defined roles and responsibilities are essential for effective data governance in healthcare IT. From executive leadership to frontline staff, the collaborative effort to establish an overarching framework promotes not only data quality and compliance but also nurtures a culture that values ethical data practices. As healthcare continues to evolve towards increasingly data-centric approaches, the collective engagement of all stakeholders will be pivotal in shaping an environment where data serves as a powerful tool for improving patient care and operational efficiency. By committing to robust data governance practices, organizations can enhance their capacity to respond to challenges, innovate in patient care delivery, and ultimately achieve better health outcomes.

5.1 Data Governance Committees

In the intricate landscape of healthcare IT, data governance has emerged as a cornerstone for maintaining the integrity, security, and utilization of health data. At the heart of effective data governance lies a structured approach to overseeing data management processes, policies, and standards. Central to this framework are data governance committees, tasked with ensuring that data practices align with the strategic objectives of healthcare organizations while complying with regulatory requirements.

Data governance committees typically comprise members from a cross-functional team, including IT staff, clinical experts, data analysts, compliance officers, and executive leadership. This diversity in membership enables a holistic perspective while making decisions that impact data governance. By convening these various stakeholders, organizations can facilitate a blend of insights and expertise that enriches discussions on data stewardship.

A primary responsibility of these committees involves establishing clear data governance policies that dictate how data is collected, stored, accessed, and shared. These policies must reflect both best practices and regulatory mandates, such as HIPAA or GDPR, that govern patient information. A well-designed policy not only protects sensitive health data but also facilitates appropriate data usage across the organization, thereby empowering clinicians and administrators to make informed decisions based on accurate and timely information.

Data governance committees also play a pivotal role in data quality assurance. Given the critical nature of health data in patient care, decisions based on inaccurate, outdated, or incomplete information can have catastrophic consequences. Establishing quality checks and standards, the committees ensure that data remains reliable and serve as an ongoing audit mechanism. This may encompass regular assessments of data collection methods, data entry protocols, and overall data lifecycle management. By instituting rigorous data quality measures, these committees help mitigate risks associated with poor data governance, including compliance failures and adverse effects on patient care.

Another vital function of these committees is oversight over data access and security. In an era when cyber threats loom large, safeguarding patient data is paramount. The governance committees must develop a framework that defines who can access data, under what conditions, and for what purposes. This includes implementing mechanisms for user authentication, data encryption, and audit trails. By establishing clear access controls and operating protocols, committees not only secure sensitive health information but also instill trust among patients who demand that their data remain confidential.

Furthermore, data governance committees are tasked with fostering a culture of data stewardship within the organization. Educating staff about the importance of data governance promotes a shared responsibility that transcends departmental boundaries. Training sessions, workshops, and regular communications ensure that all employees understand their roles in safeguarding data, adhering to governance policies, and leveraging data effectively for improved patient outcomes. Awareness initiatives also empower staff to question data practices and challenge non-compliance when necessary, promoting accountability at every level of the organization.

The evolution of data governance requires that these committees remain agile and adaptive to technological advancements and changing regulatory landscapes. For instance, the increasing incorporation of artificial intelligence and machine learning in health IT necessitates an examination of ethical considerations around data usage. Committees need to assess how algorithms use health data, ensuring compliance with ethical standards while enhancing the quality of patient care. By seeking continuous improvement, governance committees can adapt to innovations that impact data management, ensuring that healthcare organizations remain ahead of the curve.

Engaging with external stakeholders is another integral aspect of the committee's responsibilities. Collaborations with patients, providers, researchers, and regulatory bodies can deepen the understanding of data governance implications. This engagement facilitates the alignment of administrative goals with the broader healthcare ecosystem's needs, enhancing the quality of data governance practices. Active participation in industry forums or networks can also empower committees to share best practices and learn from the experiences of others, fostering a spirit of cooperation in the advancement of healthcare data governance.

Finally, success in data governance ultimately relies on measuring performance and demonstrating the value of governance initiatives. Through established key performance indicators (KPIs) and metrics, committees can assess data quality, compliance levels, and the effectiveness of governance policies. Regular reporting provides insights on progress and areas requiring further attention while reinforcing executive support for governance efforts. By showcasing the positive impact of robust data governance—such as improved patient outcomes, reduced regulatory risks, and more efficient operations—committees can champion data governance as a strategic imperative rather than a mere regulatory obligation.

In conclusion, data governance committees serve as vital enablers within the complex healthcare IT landscape, addressing the multifaceted needs of data management. By establishing policies, ensuring data quality, and promoting ethical data use, they can drive meaningful change in organizational practices. As healthcare continues to embrace technological advancements, these committees must remain vigilant and proactive, fostering a culture of collaboration, compliance, and continuous improvement. Through their stewardship, healthcare organizations can confidently navigate the complexities of data governance, positioning themselves to deliver improved patient care and uphold the trust placed in them by patients and stakeholders alike.

5.2 Data Stewards and Custodians

In the complex landscape of healthcare IT, effective data governance is critical to ensuring the integrity, privacy, and accessibility of patient information. Central to this governance framework are roles known as data stewards and custodians. Their importance cannot be overstated as they serve as the bridge between data management and compliance, focusing on the stewardship of healthcare data to maximize its value while mitigating risks.

Data stewards are the individuals responsible for the quality and integrity of data throughout its lifecycle. They play an instrumental role in defining, implementing, and enforcing data governance policies. Their responsibilities encompass a range of activities, including data quality management, metadata management, and ensuring adherence to regulatory compliance. In a healthcare context, where data accuracy can directly impact patient outcomes, the role of data stewards becomes even more critical. They must continually monitor data sets to identify discrepancies, resolve data quality issues, and maintain rigor around data definitions and standards.

A healthcare dataset, for example, consists of clinical information, financial details, and demographic data about patients. Poor data quality can lead to misdiagnosis, inappropriate treatment, or billing errors, all of which have profound implications. Data stewards must establish processes to verify the accuracy of this information regularly, utilizing methods such as validation checks or cross-referencing against external databases. Effective data stewardship ensures that healthcare providers make informed decisions based on accurate, timely information.

In addition to management and quality assurance, data stewards are tasked with the development of data standards that govern the collection, storage, and sharing of data. They need to work closely with IT departments, healthcare practitioners, and compliance officers to create a coherent framework that adheres to established regulations such as HIPAA. Through the establishment of uniform data standards, stewards facilitate seamless data sharing across different departments and systems, ultimately leading to improved continuity of care and better patient outcomes.

While data stewards focus on the governance, quality, and usage of data, data custodians occupy a different yet complementary role. Custodians are primarily responsible for the technical management and protection of data, ensuring that data systems are secure, maintainable, and resilient. Their focus lies in the infrastructure that supports data storage, retrieval, and archiving, alongside the application of necessary security protocols to protect sensitive healthcare information from breaches or unauthorized access.

In a healthcare setting, data custodians manage databases, servers, and cloud solutions. They implement access controls, encryption, and auditing tools to protect patient data. As cyber threats continue to evolve in complexity and frequency, the importance of custodians cannot be overlooked. They are tasked with ensuring compliance with cybersecurity frameworks like NIST and ISO, which dictate the necessary processes to secure healthcare data from cyberattacks. The custodian's role extends to managing backup and recovery processes, providing assurance that in the event of a data loss incident, patient data can be restored promptly.

Collaboration is essential between data stewards and custodians, as effective data governance relies on a holistic approach to securing data while maximizing its utility. The strategic alignment of these roles ensures that data management efforts are consistent, synchronized, and efficient. For instance, when launching a new health information system, data stewards may quote the requirements for data quality and compliance, while custodians focus on the technical architecture and security measures that will uphold those standards. This collaboration not only supports regulatory compliance but also fosters a culture of accountability and shared responsibility across the organization.

Stakeholder engagement is another critical dimension of their work. Data stewards and custodians must communicate effectively with various stakeholders, including clinical staff, administrative personnel, IT teams, and executive leadership. They must provide training and guidance around data governance policies while raising awareness about the significance of data integrity, security, and compliance. Clear communication and collaboration create a unified approach towards data governance.

Moreover, in a landscape consisting of constant regulatory changes, both roles require an ongoing commitment to professional development and awareness of emerging trends. Attendance at industry conferences and workshops, participation in training sessions, and engagement in relevant communities of practice are essential to staying current. This proactive engagement enables data stewards and custodians to anticipate changes in legislation or technologies that may impact their data governance framework.

Emphasizing the significance of data stewards and custodians within healthcare IT is imperative. As organizations continue to undergo digital transformations and implement advanced analytics, the infrastructure of data governance becomes ever more critical. Together, data stewards and custodians not only ensure the integrity and security of healthcare data but also enable organizations to leverage data as a strategic asset. Their efforts result in enhanced patient care, improved operational efficiency, and a stronger regulatory posture. In summary, the functions of these roles are invaluable in navigating the complexities of healthcare data management and fostering a rigorous data governance culture within healthcare IT environments.

5.3 Training and Awareness Programs

Effective data governance in healthcare IT relies heavily on comprehensive training and awareness programs. Such programs ensure that all stakeholders are equipped with the necessary knowledge and skills to manage patient data responsibly, adhering to relevant regulations and organizational policies. The ever-evolving landscape of healthcare technology, combined with the sensitive nature of patient information, underscores the need for robust training initiatives.

Training programs should initially focus on the foundational elements of data governance, including the principles of data ownership, data stewardship, and the distinctions between different types of healthcare data. Personnel need to understand the critical role that data plays in patient care, operational efficiency, and regulatory compliance. Knowledge of data governance frameworks, such as the General Data Protection Regulation (GDPR) and the Health Insurance Portability and Accountability Act (HIPAA), is essential for identifying legal obligations and institutional policies that affect the management of health information.

A successful training program utilizes a blended approach, combining online modules with in-person workshops. This hybrid model ensures that employees can learn at their own pace while also benefiting from interactive discussions and hands-on practice. Online resources can cover theoretical aspects and case studies, while workshops can facilitate scenario-based training, where participants engage in real-life situations that they may encounter in their roles. This approach not only aids in knowledge retention but also helps develop critical thinking skills necessary for effective decision-making.

Role-specific training is another vital aspect. Different groups within the healthcare organization—ranging from medical practitioners to administrative staff—require tailored training that addresses their unique responsibilities and the corresponding data governance challenges they face. For instance, clinical staff should be well-versed in the ways data governance affects patient care, such as understanding patient consent management and the importance of accurate data entry for clinical decision-making. On the other hand, administrative personnel need to be knowledgeable about compliance and risk management regarding data handling and reporting.

Engaging employees through simulations and interactive exercises is essential to solidify their understanding. Simulations can replicate data handling scenarios, allowing individuals to practice their response to common data governance issues, such as data breaches or unauthorized access. Interactive learning encourages teamwork and collaboration among departments, fostering a culture of shared responsibility for data governance. This cultural shift is crucial because it mitigates the silo mentality, ensuring that all employees recognize that data governance is a collective effort rather than the sole responsibility of an IT team.

In addition to initial training, continuous learning initiatives are pivotal to keeping staff updated on emerging threats, technological advancements, and regulatory changes that could impact data governance. Regular refresher courses, newsletters, and seminars can keep the workforce informed about the latest best practices and innovations in the field of data governance. Establishing a dedicated data governance committee that includes representatives from various departments can also help facilitate ongoing education. This committee can serve as a resource for addressing questions or concerns, promoting knowledge sharing, and ensuring alignment across the organization.

Awareness programs should extend to engage all stakeholders, including patients and their families. While healthcare organizations often concentrate on training internal staff, patient awareness is equally crucial. Patients should be educated about how their data is collected, stored, and shared, as well as their rights under data protection laws. Clear communication about what steps the organization takes to safeguard their information can enhance patient trust—a vital component in fostering collaborative patient-provider relationships.

Furthermore, organizations should leverage technology to enhance training and awareness efforts. Utilizing Learning Management Systems (LMS) equips organizations with the tools necessary to track progress, gather data on training effectiveness, and offer personalized learning paths. Organizations can also explore incorporating gamification elements to make the training process more engaging. Leaderboards, rewards systems, and interactive quizzes can encourage healthy competition and increase participation among employees.

Evaluating the effectiveness of training and awareness programs is an essential step in the continuous improvement process. Feedback mechanisms, such as surveys or post-training assessments, can help organizations understand the impact of their initiatives and identify areas for improvement. Regular audits and assessments of data management practices are vital for ensuring compliance with governance standards, as these evaluations can lead to actionable insights that inform future training needs.

In conclusion, the implementation of comprehensive training and awareness programs is paramount in establishing a robust data governance framework within healthcare IT. Such initiatives equip every stakeholder with the necessary knowledge and skills to handle data responsibly, secure patient trust, and fulfill compliance obligations. Ultimately, fostering a culture of data stewardship enables healthcare organizations to leverage data as a strategic asset while safeguarding the privacy and security of patient information in an era of rapid technological advancement.

Chapter 6: Risk Management and Compliance Strategies

Effective management of risk and adherence to compliance standards are paramount in the realm of healthcare IT, where the convergence of patient data, technology, and regulatory frameworks creates a complex landscape. Healthcare organizations face myriad challenges that can jeopardize the integrity and security of sensitive information. Therefore, robust risk management and compliance strategies are essential components of data governance frameworks, serving not only to protect patient data but also to bolster organizational resilience.

Risk assessment is the keystone of a well-crafted risk management strategy. It involves identifying potential threats to the confidentiality, integrity, and availability of data and systems. In healthcare IT, risks can emerge from various sources including human error, system failures, and cyber threats. The increasing prevalence of ransomware attacks has highlighted the vulnerability of healthcare organizations to sophisticated cybercriminal tactics. Therefore, conducting thorough, periodic risk assessments is critical for identifying vulnerabilities and preparing proactive strategies to mitigate potential impacts.

Once risks are identified, organizations must prioritize them based on their potential impact and the likelihood of occurrence. This prioritization allows healthcare IT leaders to allocate resources effectively, focusing on the most pressing threats to their data governance framework. Developing a risk matrix can facilitate this process by allowing teams to visualize risk levels and make informed decisions regarding risk mitigation strategies.

In tandem with risk assessment is the development of effective compliance strategies. Healthcare IT is predominantly influenced by a framework of regulations including the Health Insurance Portability and Accountability Act (HIPAA), the Health Information Technology for Economic and Clinical Health (HITECH) Act, and various state-level regulations. Compliance with these mandates is essential not only to avoid hefty penalties but also to ensure the protection of patient rights and data integrity.

A foundational step in establishing compliance strategies is to foster a culture of compliance within the organization. This culture must be cultivated through ongoing training and education for all employees on compliance requirements and best practices in data governance. Regular training sessions, simulated phishing attacks, and reminders of the regulatory landscape can engage personnel and instill a sense of accountability. Employees should understand their roles in protecting patient data and the consequences of non-compliance, thereby enhancing the overall security posture of the organization.

Moreover, appointing a compliance officer or a dedicated team focused on compliance matters can streamline this process. A compliance officer serves as a liaison between various departments, ensuring that they adhere to laws and policies pertaining to data governance. This individual is responsible for staying abreast of regulatory changes and translating these into actionable compliance measures across the organization.

A critical aspect of compliance strategies is the implementation of robust policies and procedures around data access and sharing. These policies should govern who has access to sensitive information, how that information is stored, and the conditions under which it can be shared. Data minimization principles should be embraced, ensuring that only the minimum necessary information for a specified purpose is collected and accessed. Such policies not only comply with regulations but also reduce the attack surface by limiting the amount of vulnerable data available.

Another effective compliance strategy is the implementation of technological safeguards such as encryption, user authentication, and access controls. Encryption mitigates the risk of data breaches, ensuring that even if data is intercepted, it remains unreadable without the proper decryption keys. Strong user authentication processes, including multi-factor authentication, further enhance security by limiting access to authorized personnel only.

Incident response planning is also a crucial element of risk management within healthcare IT environments. Despite the best prevention strategies, incidents can and will occur. An incident response plan outlines structured procedures for addressing and mitigating the effects of data breaches, system downtimes, or other disruptions. Key components of an incident response plan include identification of the incident, containment measures, eradication of the threat, recovery processes, and post-incident analysis. Regular testing of the incident response plan allows organizations to refine their responses and adapt to evolving technological threats.

Finally, continuous monitoring and auditing of data governance practices are vital components of risk management and compliance strategies. These ongoing evaluations ensure that policies remain effective and that any changes in the regulatory landscape are reflected in the organization's practices. Automated monitoring tools can track data access and modifications, alerting administrators to suspicious activities in real time. Regular audits, both internal and external, assess adherence to policies and help identify areas for improvement.

In summary, the landscape of healthcare IT demands a multifaceted approach to risk management and compliance strategies. By conducting thorough risk assessments, fostering a culture of compliance, implementing robust technical safeguards, and maintaining ongoing monitoring practices, healthcare organizations can effectively navigate the complexities of data governance. Such proactive measures not only protect patient data but also enhance the organization's overall integrity and trust within the healthcare ecosystem.

6.1 Identifying Data Compliance Risks

Effective data governance in healthcare IT is critical for ensuring that sensitive patient information is handled responsibly and ethically. This landscape is becoming increasingly complex and fraught with compliance risks, particularly as healthcare organizations increasingly rely on digital health records, telemedicine, and artificial intelligence. Identifying compliance risks in data governance is fundamental for healthcare providers, as non-compliance can result in severe penalties, damage to reputation, and loss of patient trust.

To commence the identification of compliance risks, it is essential to understand the regulatory framework governing healthcare data. The Health Insurance Portability and Accountability Act (HIPAA) in the United States, for example, sets stringent standards for the protection of patient information. Organizations must ensure that all electronic protected health information (ePHI) is safeguarded against unauthorized access and breaches. Thus, compliance risks arise whenever there is inadequate protection or oversight of ePHI, often stemming from insufficient employee training or lack of robust security protocols.

Data sharing and interoperability between healthcare entities further complicate compliance. As organizations collaborate to improve patient care and streamline operations, they increase the likelihood of data transfers that may not adhere to compliance rules. Misalignment around consent, data ownership, and the legal implications of sharing data across state lines or with third parties can create significant risk. Additionally, healthcare providers must be vigilant in recognizing that data shared with vendors or partners may expose them to new vulnerabilities, especially if third parties do not adhere to the same compliance standards.

Failures in data classification can also pose compliance risks. Healthcare data is often diverse and categorized differently across departments. Without a robust data classification framework, organizations can find themselves unable to ascertain which information is sensitive, necessitating a higher level of protection under legislation like HIPAA. This lack of clarity may lead to improper handling of data, exposing sensitive information to unauthorized users. It is pivotal for healthcare IT professionals to implement comprehensive data classification strategies to ensure that the most sensitive information is appropriately managed.

Another area of risk is data retention and disposal. Healthcare organizations are required to retain patient records for certain periods as mandated by state and federal regulations. However, organizations must also have defined strategies for safely disposing of data that is no longer needed. Failure to securely delete or destroy this information can result in unintentional data leaks or breaches, which can lead to severe regulatory consequences. A clear data lifecycle management policy is required to mitigate these risks—an initiative that should involve training for all personnel on data handling practices through its lifecycle.

Within this domain, the human element remains a pivotal factor in compliance risk management. Employee actions (or inactions) can lead to significant vulnerabilities, whether through social engineering attacks, negligent handling of sensitive data, or insufficient reporting of security incidents. Ongoing training and a culture of compliance can serve as powerful tools against these risks. By cultivating an environment in which employees feel empowered to report security issues, or that fosters awareness about data breaches, organizations can mitigate risks associated with human error.

Responding to potential data breaches forms a crucial component of an overall risk management strategy. Healthcare organizations must have comprehensive incident response plans that outline the steps to be taken in the event of a breach, including notifying affected individuals, reporting the incident to regulators, and taking remedial action. A failure to respond appropriately can exacerbate compliance breaches and lead to greater penalties. Regular testing and updating of incident response plans are critical to ensure that they remain effective against evolving threats.

Advanced technologies, such as artificial intelligence and machine learning, hold both promise and peril in the healthcare IT landscape. While these technologies can enhance patient care and streamline operations, they can also introduce compliance risks if not used responsibly. Automated systems are often designed to streamline data processes, but if they misinterpret data classification or allow sensitive information to be disseminated inappropriately, the potential for compliance failure increases. Therefore, healthcare IT must not only be innovative but also responsible. Compliance frameworks should evolve in alignment with these technologies, ensuring proper governance and control mechanisms are in place.

Moreover, mapping data flows within an organization can help identify areas where compliance risks are prevalent. Health organizations frequently generate, process, and share vast volumes of data. By creating a comprehensive map of data flows, organizations can identify which departments are most exposed to compliance risks and subsequently implement targeted controls. By mapping all data movement—internally and externally—organizations can enforce stricter access controls and better manage data lifecycle protocols.

In conclusion, identifying data compliance risks within healthcare IT necessitates a proactive and multi-faceted approach. From understanding regulatory obligations to fostering a culture of compliance and accountability, organizations must engage multiple strategies to ensure that risks are adequately recognized and managed. As healthcare technology continues to advance, so too will the nuances of compliance, making it imperative for healthcare organizations to remain vigilant and adaptive in the face of evolving threats. By doing so, healthcare organizations not only protect themselves from potential regulatory repercussions but also enhance the quality of care delivered to patients, thus preserving the integrity of the healthcare system as a whole.

6.2 Mitigation Strategies for NonCompliance

Compliance with data governance regulations in healthcare IT is a pressing concern, especially with the continuous evolution of technology and data management practices. The ramifications of noncompliance can be severe, encompassing financial penalties, reputational damage, and compromised patient trust. Consequently, organizations must adopt proactive mitigation strategies to address potential noncompliance issues before they escalate.

First and foremost, one of the core strategies for mitigating noncompliance involves establishing a robust framework for data governance. This framework should articulate the roles, responsibilities, and processes necessary for effective data management across the organization. By clearly defining ownership and accountability, organizations can ensure that every stakeholder understands their obligations concerning data handling, storage, and sharing. It is crucial to engage all levels of the organization, from executive leadership to front-line staff, in this framework to cultivate a culture of compliance.

Training and education form another pillar of a comprehensive mitigation strategy. Regular training sessions tailored to various staff roles ensure that employees grasp both the importance of data governance and the specific regulations that pertain to their functions. Educational programs should go beyond basic compliance checklists; they should foster critical thinking about ethical data use, the implications of breaches, and the importance of patient privacy. As technology evolves, continuous learning opportunities will keep staff informed about updates in legislation, technology, or best practices, thus reducing the risk of error or oversight that could lead to noncompliance.

Moreover, organizations must invest in advanced monitoring and auditing tools that offer real-time insights into data governance practices. These tools can identify noncompliance risks before they materialize into critical issues. By deploying analytics, organizations can gain visibility into data access, usage patterns, and anomalies that might indicate potential breaches. Regular audits, both internal and external, serve as a validation mechanism for compliance efforts and can help identify gaps in policies, processes, or technologies that need to be addressed. These proactive measures ensure that organizations remain vigilant and responsive to potential compliance challenges.

In addition to monitoring and auditing, fostering a culture of open communication is essential for mitigating noncompliance. Creating channels for staff to discuss concerns related to data governance without fear of retaliation encourages accountability and transparency. Whistleblower protections and anonymous reporting systems can empower employees to highlight potential compliance issues early on, allowing organizations to act swiftly to rectify such matters before they escalate into more significant problems. This culture not only safeguards data compliance but also enhances employee morale and trust in the organization.

Furthermore, it is critical to integrate compliance considerations into the organization's technology strategy. As healthcare organizations adopt new IT systems or migrate data to cloud platforms, governance mechanisms must be embedded from the outset. This involves evaluating software vendors for their adherence to data governance standards and ensuring that any technology solutions align with regulatory requirements such as HIPAA and GDPR. A rigorous vendor selection process that prioritizes compliance and security helps mitigate risks associated with third-party data handling, thus reinforcing the organization's overall compliance posture.

Another effective approach to mitigate noncompliance involves collaborative partnerships across the healthcare ecosystem. Engaging with peers, industry groups, and regulatory bodies fosters a collaborative approach to shared compliance challenges. Organizations can benefit from benchmarking against best practices and learning from the experiences of others in the field. Participation in industry forums and committees facilitates the exchange of knowledge and resources, ultimately enhancing the collective understanding of compliance requirements within the sector. This external perspective can also illuminate emerging trends or regulatory changes that may necessitate adjustments in data governance practices.

The role of leadership in fostering a compliance-oriented environment cannot be overstated. Executive buy-in is often the linchpin for effective data governance initiatives. Leaders must model compliance behaviors and embed these values into the organizational ethos. By championing compliance initiatives, allocating resources to support governance efforts, and prioritizing data ethics in decision-making, leadership sets the tone for the entire organization. Their commitment not only drives compliance initiatives but also inspires all employees to uphold the highest standards of data stewardship.

Finally, organizations should maintain a proactive stance through regular risk assessments that identify compliance vulnerabilities and assess the effectiveness of existing governance protocols. These assessments should not be a one-time exercise but rather an ongoing process that actively engages stakeholders from various disciplines to ensure a comprehensive understanding of compliance risks. By embracing a dynamic risk management approach, organizations are better equipped to adapt to regulatory changes and quickly mitigate emerging compliance threats.

In conclusion, the landscape of healthcare IT is fraught with challenges related to data governance and compliance. By adopting a multi-faceted approach that encompasses a robust governance framework, continuous training, advanced monitoring, open communication, technology integration, collaborative partnerships, strong leadership, and proactive risk assessments, organizations can significantly mitigate the risks associated with noncompliance. As the industry continues to evolve, these strategies will be vital for ensuring that healthcare organizations uphold their ethical obligations and safeguard patient data effectively.

6.3 Incident Reporting and Response Protocols

In the increasingly digitized landscape of healthcare IT, incident reporting and response protocols play a pivotal role in safeguarding sensitive patient data and ensuring the integrity of health information systems. The protection of personal health information is not merely a regulatory obligation but a fundamental aspect of maintaining patient trust and enhancing healthcare outcomes. Hence, robust incident reporting and response frameworks are vital components of comprehensive data governance strategies.

The first step in effective incident reporting involves the establishment of clear definitions and categories for possible incidents. These can range from data breaches and unauthorized access to system failures and accidental disclosures. Organizations must differentiate between incidents that pose minimal risk and those that could have devastating consequences. This categorization enables a more effective response strategy and resource allocation. A well-articulated framework enhances awareness among employees about the types of incidents that must be reported, thereby fostering a culture of vigilance.

Once incidents are identified and reported, swift and efficient response mechanisms must be activated. This begins with the formation of a dedicated response team composed of IT professionals, data governance officers, legal advisors, and communication specialists. This multidisciplinary approach ensures that all aspects of the incident are managed effectively, from technical containment to legal compliance. The response team should leverage a predefined incident response plan that delineates specific procedures and roles, allowing for a coordinated and timely response.

Communication is integral to the incident response process. Stakeholders, including employees, patients, and regulatory bodies, must be informed promptly and accurately about incidents. Transparent communication fosters trust and accountability, particularly in healthcare settings where the repercussions of data breaches can significantly strain patient relationships. Moreover, organizations must ensure compliance with relevant regulations, such as the Health Insurance Portability and Accountability Act (HIPAA) in the United States, which necessitates timely notification of affected individuals in the event of a breach involving their personal health information.

In conjunction with these response protocols, organizations must also implement robust monitoring and analysis systems to track incidents over time. By maintaining a comprehensive incident log, healthcare organizations can identify patterns and trends, enabling them to refine their security measures and response strategies proactively. Regular audits and assessments of these incidents allow for continual improvement in incident management and can inform future data governance policies.

Training and awareness programs serve as preventive measures that can significantly reduce the likelihood of incidents. Ongoing education for all employees about data governance principles, regulatory requirements, and reporting protocols is essential. These programs should not only focus on compliance but also emphasize the importance of a proactive security culture. Employees must feel empowered to report concerns and incidents without fear of reprisal. A non-punitive reporting atmosphere encourages a more secure environment, decreasing the risk of incidents wreaking havoc on systems.

Data governance also necessitates robust technical controls that support incident detection and reporting efforts. Techniques such as intrusion detection systems (IDS), data loss prevention (DLP) solutions, and regular system audits act as crucial line of defenses. By integrating these technologies, healthcare organizations can enhance their ability to detect irregularities and respond to incidents in real-time. These technical measures must, however, be complemented by appropriate governance policies and user training to ensure an all-encompassing approach to data security.

Post-incident analysis is another crucial phase in the incident reporting and response cycle, allowing organizations to learn from each occurrence. Conducting a thorough root cause analysis facilitates the identification of systemic vulnerabilities and inadequacies in existing protocols. By understanding the incident's context and consequences, healthcare organizations can implement better security measures and training, thereby enriching their data governance framework. This iterative improvement process reflects a commitment to sustainability in healthcare IT practices, with data protection evolving as new threats emerge.

Furthermore, collaboration among healthcare organizations can enhance incident response capabilities. By participating in information-sharing networks, organizations can stay abreast of emerging threats and best practices in incident management. Collaborative efforts can range from sharing anonymized incident reports to participating in joint training exercises and workshops. Such alliances enable smaller organizations, which may lack substantial resources, to benefit from the collective knowledge and tools of larger entities.

To synthesize, the landscape of healthcare IT demands a meticulous approach to incident reporting and response that underpins effective data governance. Establishing a structured reporting framework, assembling multidisciplinary response teams, fostering transparent communication, and committing to continuous learning are critical elements in combating data risks. By integrating these components into a unified strategy, healthcare organizations not only protect sensitive information but also reinforce their commitment to patient safety and trust. Ultimately, the overarching goal is to create a resilient data governance environment that not only responds to incidents but prevents them from occurring in the first place, ensuring the integrity and confidentiality of healthcare data in an era of rapid technological advancement.

Chapter 7: Implementing a Data Governance Framework

Data governance within the healthcare IT landscape represents a critical aspect of the management of information assets. It encompasses the structures, policies, and technologies that control how data is collected, stored, and shared, ensuring that data integrity, privacy, and compliance with legal regulations are maintained. Implementing a comprehensive data governance framework is vital for healthcare organizations aiming to achieve operational efficiency while safeguarding sensitive information.

The first step in developing a robust data governance framework involves establishing a strategic vision supported by organizational leadership. This commitment must transcend mere compliance; it should reflect a genuine intention to leverage data as a strategic asset for improved patient outcomes and organizational efficiency. Healthcare organizations should develop a data governance charter that outlines the goals, principles, and scope of their governance initiatives. This charter must be aligned with the overall strategic objectives of the organization and requires input from various stakeholders, including clinical staff, IT teams, and compliance officers. Such collaboration ensures that the framework adequately addresses the unique needs and challenges of an interdisciplinary environment.

Following the establishment of a governance charter, the formation of a data governance board is essential. This board, composed of representatives from key departments such as clinical operations, compliance, IT, and data analytics, serves as the decision-making body, fostering accountability and establishing clear lines of authority. The board's responsibilities should revolve around defining data governance policies and standards, resolving conflicts over data ownership, and prioritizing data-related projects based on organizational needs. The representation of diverse departments within the board enhances collective insight into data usage and fosters a culture of data stewardship throughout the organization.

In parallel, it is crucial to delineate data stewardship roles and responsibilities across the organization. Appointing data stewards in various departments reinforces the notion that data governance is a shared responsibility rather than a siloed function within IT. Data stewards are tasked with overseeing data quality and integrity in their specific domains, ensuring that data entry, management, and dissemination adhere to established standards. By embedding stewardship roles into departmental functions, organizations can cultivate a data-driven culture, where all staff members recognize the importance of maintaining data accuracy and security in their daily tasks.

A successful data governance framework also requires the establishment of policies for data quality management. Healthcare organizations must implement processes to regularly assess and improve data quality by addressing issues such as accuracy, completeness, consistency, timeliness, and relevance. These policies should include data validation rules, audit procedures, and mechanisms for reporting data quality issues. Regular training sessions and communication campaigns can further promote awareness and understanding of data quality standards among staff, ensuring that everyone plays a role in achieving data excellence.

Data privacy and security are paramount in the healthcare sector, necessitating the incorporation of regulatory compliance into the data governance framework. The framework should not only comply with established standards such as the Health Insurance Portability and Accountability Act (HIPAA) but also evolve in response to emerging regulations and technologies. It is vital to establish processes for data access control, encryption, and secure sharing of sensitive information across the organization. Healthcare IT departments must work closely with compliance officers to conduct regular risk assessments and audits aimed at identifying vulnerabilities in data management practices. Such proactive measures not only mitigate risks but also foster trust among patients and stakeholders.

Implementing effective data lifecycle management strategies is another cornerstone of a solid governance framework. This involves defining how data is captured, used, archived, and disposed of within the organization. Clear guidelines pertaining to data retention policies must be established to ensure compliance with legal and regulatory requirements. Organizations should employ technology solutions that facilitate automated data classification, retention schedules, and secure disposal methods. Emphasizing data lifecycle management will not only optimize resource allocation but also improve the organization's ability to extract valuable insights from datasets.

Training and education form a crucial component of a successful data governance initiative. Staff at all levels must be equipped with the knowledge and skills necessary to understand their roles within the data governance framework. Continuous professional development programs should be designed to keep healthcare employees abreast of best practices in data management, new technologies, and changing regulations. By fostering an environment of continuous learning, organizations position themselves to adapt to the evolving data landscape.

Finally, organizations must measure the effectiveness of their data governance framework through ongoing evaluation and adjustment. Key performance indicators (KPIs) should be established to gauge various aspects of data governance, including data quality metrics, compliance adherence rates, and user satisfaction. Regular feedback from stakeholders can provide insights into areas of improvement, enabling organizations to refine their data governance strategies continually.

In conclusion, the implementation of a data governance framework within healthcare IT is a multifaceted endeavor that requires strategic planning, collaboration, and commitment from all levels of the organization. By establishing a governance structure, defining roles and responsibilities, managing data quality, ensuring compliance with regulations, and investing in training and continuous evaluation, healthcare organizations can unlock the full potential of their data. This proactive approach not only enhances operational efficiency but also contributes to superior patient care, reinforcing data as an invaluable asset in the healthcare ecosystem.

7.1 Framework Design and Development

The integration of 7.1 Framework Design in the realm of Data Governance within Healthcare IT elevates the management of health data from a mere compliance necessity to a strategic advantage. In an industry where data is both abundant and sensitive, establishing robust governance constructs is essential to ensure that information is accurate, secure, and utilized effectively. The 7.1 Framework facilitates a systematic approach to data governance by presenting a modular and adaptable structure that healthcare organizations can tailor to their specific needs.

At the heart of the framework is the understanding that data governance encompasses the policies, procedures, and standards necessary for effective data management. Healthcare organizations must establish a common language around data by operationalizing key terms and definitions that resonate across departments. This shared understanding underpins data integrity while fostering collaboration that transcends siloed functionalities.

A crucial component of the 7.1 Framework is defining clear roles and responsibilities. Designating data governance officers and data stewards is imperative for instigating accountability within the organization. These individuals become the custodians of data quality, ensuring that everyone from clinicians to administrative staff understands the protocols for data entry, management, and usage. The establishment of cross-functional data governance committees further consolidates authority, allowing an ongoing dialogue regarding data practices and evolving needs.

In healthcare, regulatory compliance is non-negotiable. The 7.1 Framework aligns data governance efforts with existing laws and regulations, such as HIPAA (Health Insurance Portability and Accountability Act) and other pertinent guidelines. By integrating compliance into the backbone of data governance, healthcare organizations can reduce their risk of liability while simultaneously enhancing their data management practices. This alignment also positions organizations to respond more swiftly to regulatory changes, ensuring that governance practices remain relevant and actionable.

The framework advocates a strategic approach towards data stewardship, particularly regarding the lifecycle management of data. Healthcare entities must recognize that data does not merely exist as static information waiting to be processed; it flows through various stages—collection, storage, sharing, and archiving. Each stage presents distinct challenges and opportunities for governance intervention. For instance, during the data collection phase, the emphasis must be placed on capturing relevant and high-quality data at the point of care. Tools such as electronic health record (EHR) systems must be configured to minimize user errors while promoting comprehensive data capture.

The aspect of data quality management ties directly into the architecture of the 7.1 Framework. Healthcare organizations must develop metrics to evaluate data quality continually. Here, the significance of data accuracy, completeness, consistency, timeliness, and relevance cannot be overstated. Without established benchmarks, organizations may struggle to ensure that their data is fit for purpose. Regular audits and assessments should be embedded within the governance strategy, empowering organizations to proactively manage and rectify data issues.

Furthermore, the framework emphasizes data security and privacy—elements crucial to maintaining stakeholder trust. In an industry rife with cyber threats and breaches, adopting a risk management approach to data governance is vital. Organizations must implement stringent access controls and encryption to protect sensitive medical records. Additionally, training staff on recognizing phishing attempts and maintaining confidentiality can drastically reduce vulnerabilities. A culture of security awareness becomes an intrinsic part of the data governance landscape.

Collaboration across departments widens the scope of data governance, promoting interoperability within healthcare systems. The 7.1 Framework encourages organizations to break down data silos to facilitate data sharing while ensuring that proper governance practices are upheld. With scaled interoperability, organizations can enhance patient care outcomes through comprehensive data exchange, ultimately allowing for more informed decision-making at both clinical and administrative levels.

Moreover, leveraging advanced analytics and technologies such as artificial intelligence (AI) can transform how organizations interact with data. The 7.1 Framework promotes exploring innovative data analytics tools to derive insights and improve patient care. However, organizations must be cognizant of ethical considerations and biases inherent in AI algorithms. The framework advises consistent evaluation of algorithms against governance standards to ensure they promote equitable healthcare access and decision-making.

Finally, continuous improvement is pivotal within the framework. Data governance is not a static endeavor; it requires regular feedback loops to adapt to the dynamic healthcare landscape. Organizations must solicit input from various stakeholders, including healthcare providers, patients, and regulatory bodies, to assess the efficacy of existing governance strategies and identify areas for enhancement. This iterative process fosters a culture of agility that can respond to shifts in data management needs and emerging healthcare trends.

In summary, the 7.1 Framework Design and Development provides a robust template for healthcare organizations aiming to navigate the intricacies of data governance effectively. By clearly defining roles, ensuring compliance, managing data quality, securing sensitive information, promoting collaboration, embracing analytics, and fostering continuous improvement, healthcare IT systems can ensure that data governance not only safeguards patient information but also advances organizational objectives. With the proper implementation of the framework, data governance becomes a cornerstone of high-caliber healthcare delivery, ultimately improving patient outcomes and institutional efficiency.

7.2 Integration with Existing Processes

Data governance is essential for healthcare organizations seeking to maximize the value of their data assets while ensuring compliance with regulations and maintaining patient trust. Integrating data governance frameworks with existing processes in healthcare IT not only reinforces data management practices but also optimizes workflows, enhances decision-making, and facilitates regulatory adherence. This integration is vital for creating a culture of accountability, supporting the interoperability of health information systems, and fostering a data-driven mindset among stakeholders.

One of the primary challenges in integrating data governance within current processes is the complex landscape of healthcare IT, which encompasses diverse systems, platforms, and workflows. To achieve a seamless integration, organizations must first assess their existing processes. This assessment includes mapping out data flows, identifying key stakeholders, and evaluating the tools currently in use. By understanding the existing framework, healthcare organizations can pinpoint areas where data governance practices can be systematically incorporated, ensuring that the governance model complements and enhances workflows rather than disrupting them.

Stakeholder engagement is crucial in this integration process. Data governance initiatives require input from a variety of stakeholders, including clinicians, IT professionals, compliance officers, and administrators. Engaging these stakeholders ensures that the governance framework is not only practical but also aligns with organizational objectives. Moreover, involving diverse perspectives fosters a sense of ownership and accountability among team members, which is critical for the successful implementation of data governance practices. Training sessions, workshops, and regular communication can facilitate stakeholder involvement, allowing organizations to bridge the gap between governance policies and operational realities.

A key aspect of effective data governance integration is the establishment of standardized data management protocols. Standardization reduces variability and enhances the quality of data across the organization. For example, implementing consistent data entry guidelines can help minimize discrepancies and improve data accuracy, thereby facilitating better clinical decision-making and reporting. Additionally, standardizing metadata management ensures compatibility across different systems, promoting interoperability and simplifying data exchanges. By embedding these standardized protocols within existing processes, organizations can ensure that data governance becomes an integral part of daily operations rather than a separate initiative.

Another critical element of successful integration is the incorporation of data stewardship roles within existing processes. Data stewards take on the responsibility of overseeing data quality, ensuring adherence to governance policies, and serving as liaisons between the IT department and clinical staff. By appointing data stewards, healthcare organizations can foster a culture of data ownership and accountability. Stewards can provide valuable insight into how best to align data governance with clinical workflows, thereby enhancing the usability of health data while ensuring compliance with regulations. The presence of dedicated personnel also facilitates ongoing monitoring and maintenance of data governance practices, which is essential for long-term sustainability.

Technology plays a pivotal role in the integration of data governance within existing healthcare IT processes. Organizations must leverage advanced technologies, such as data analytics and informatics tools, to enable real-time monitoring and reporting of data quality metrics. By integrating these technologies into the governance framework, healthcare institutions can automate the tracking of data integrity and compliance, thereby reducing the burden on staff and allowing for faster issue resolution. Additionally, employing machine learning algorithms can assist in identifying patterns and anomalies within health data, prompting more informed decision-making aligned with governance objectives.

Ensuring compliance with relevant regulations is another critical facet of embedding data governance within healthcare IT processes. The healthcare sector is subject to stringent regulatory requirements, including HIPAA and HITECH, which mandate the protection of patient information and the ethical use of health data. Integrating data governance practices within existing compliance processes mitigates the risk of regulatory violations and enhances overall organizational integrity. Regular audits, adherence monitoring, and compliance training can be seamlessly intertwined with data governance initiatives, reinforcing the importance of data protection and ethical information use across all levels of the organization.

Lastly, fostering a culture of continuous improvement is essential for the successful integration of data governance with existing healthcare IT processes. Monitoring the effectiveness and impact of governance practices should be an ongoing endeavor. Organizations ought to establish key performance indicators (KPIs) to measure the success of data governance initiatives in relation to operational efficiencies, data quality, and regulatory compliance. Regular feedback loops that incorporate input from stakeholders can drive iterative improvements, ensuring that the governance framework evolves alongside organizational goals and technological advancements.

In conclusion, integrating data governance with existing processes in healthcare IT is a multifaceted endeavor that necessitates a strategic approach, stakeholder involvement, technological integration, and an unwavering commitment to compliance and continuous improvement. By systematically embedding governance practices into the fabric of day-to-day operations, healthcare organizations can enhance data quality, optimize workflows, and support a culture of accountability. As the healthcare landscape continues to evolve, the integration of robust data governance frameworks will be paramount in ensuring the ethical, efficient, and effective management of health data—ultimately enhancing patient care and organizational efficacy.

7.3 Measuring Effectiveness and Continuous Improvement

In the rapidly evolving landscape of healthcare IT, the effective management of data through comprehensive governance frameworks is crucial for ensuring both operational efficiency and compliance with regulatory mandates. As organizations strive to harness the power of data to improve patient outcomes, it becomes imperative to adopt clear methodologies for measuring effectiveness and fostering continuous improvement within their data governance initiatives.

A pivotal starting point in assessing the effectiveness of data governance frameworks lies in establishing clear metrics and key performance indicators (KPIs). These metrics should be aligned with the organization's strategic objectives, encompassing aspects such as data quality, accessibility, security, and compliance. For instance, organizations might measure the percentage of data entries that meet predefined quality standards, the frequency of data access attempts logged, or compliance incidents reported. By quantifying these elements, healthcare IT leaders can gain a deeper understanding of where their governance initiatives are succeeding and where deficiencies may exist.

Data quality stands at the forefront of any governance strategy, as institutional decision-making relies heavily on the integrity of data. Regular audits can be implemented to analyze data accuracy, completeness, consistency, and timeliness. For example, using data profiling tools not only helps in identifying discrepancies but also aids in establishing a baseline for continuous monitoring. Once baseline metrics are established, organizations can track improvements over time, ensuring accountability and promoting a culture of quality within the data governance framework.

Access controls and security protocols must also be monitored closely to mitigate risks associated with data breaches and unauthorized access. Organizations can evaluate the effectiveness of their access control mechanisms by tracking user access logs, identifying anomalies, and assessing incident response times. Furthermore, incorporating feedback loops involving stakeholders across various departments reinforces a collaborative approach to security, allowing for the identification of gaps in training and communication regarding data use.

Compliance with regulatory frameworks, such as HIPAA and GDPR, is another domain where effectiveness measurements are critical. Organizations should develop a compliance dashboard that aggregates relevant information—such as training completion rates, audit findings, and reported incidents—enabling them to visualize their compliance status. By continually assessing compliance metrics, healthcare organizations can proactively address vulnerabilities and implement corrective actions, thereby fostering a culture of accountability and ensuring adherence to legal mandates.

The shift from traditional data governance models to agile frameworks introduces opportunities for rapid evaluation and iterative improvements. Agile methodologies foster a spirit of experimentation, allowing organizations to pilot process changes on a smaller scale before full implementation. By employing techniques such as A/B testing, organizations can assess the impact of various governance strategies on data quality and operational efficiency. Incorporating stakeholder feedback in these pilot phases not only enhances the relevance of governance practices but also promotes buy-in from critical users.

Continuous improvement should be viewed not merely as a series of isolated initiatives but as an overarching philosophy that permeates the organization's culture. Establishing regular training sessions and workshops for staff involved in data governance—ranging from data stewards to IT personnel—ensures that all team members are equipped with the latest best practices and tools. This emphasis on education empowers employees to take ownership of data quality and governance processes, instilling a sense of responsibility that transcends departmental boundaries.

Investment in advanced technologies—including artificial intelligence and machine learning—presents a transformative potential for data governance in healthcare. These technologies can automate data monitoring processes, flagging inconsistencies and compliance risks in real time. By harnessing the capabilities of predictive analytics, organizations can anticipate potential data governance challenges and develop proactive strategies to mitigate them, thereby embedding a forward-thinking approach into their governance framework.

To facilitate a sustainable approach to measuring effectiveness and continuous improvement, data governance leaders should prioritize the establishment of a cross-functional governance committee. This committee, comprising stakeholders from IT, compliance, clinical operations, and data management, can champion governance initiatives, oversee performance evaluations, and guide the organization through the complexities of regulatory landscapes. By engaging diverse perspectives, organizations can ensure that their data governance frameworks are comprehensive and resilient.

Furthermore, embracing data stewardship as a core principle can enhance the overall governance structure. Designating specific roles responsible for the lifecycle management of data—from creation and storage to sharing and deletion—ensures that individuals are vested in the quality and security of the data. Accountability at these levels is essential for maintaining a robust governance framework that is responsive to both emerging challenges and strategic opportunities.

Lastly, continuous monitoring and adaptation of governance strategies should be underpinned by an open feedback loop, incorporating insights and observations from all levels of the organization. Regular review cycles enable organizations to pivot when necessary, ensuring that governance frameworks remain aligned with evolving technologies, regulations, and organizational goals.

In conclusion, effective measurement and continuous improvement in data governance strategies are foundational to maximizing the potential of healthcare IT. By establishing relevant metrics, promoting collaboration, utilizing advanced technologies, and embedding a culture of accountability, organizations can navigate the complexities of data governance with agility and resilience. These efforts will ultimately lead to enhanced data quality, better compliance, and improved patient outcomes—critical success factors in the contemporary healthcare environment.

Chapter 8: Technology and Tools for Data Governance

In the complex landscape of healthcare IT, effective data governance is paramount for ensuring the privacy, security, and quality of health information. The advancements in technology and the availability of specialized tools have dramatically transformed how organizations manage their data governance frameworks. These technological innovations facilitate not only compliance with regulatory requirements but also enhance organizational efficiency and decision-making capabilities.

At the core of effective data governance is the need for a robust data management strategy that is fortified by technology. Data governance tools often encompass data discovery, cataloging, quality assessment, and lineage tracking. They provide a central repository for all data assets, allowing organizations to maintain an inventory that meets regulatory requirements while enabling data-driven decision-making. For instance, data cataloging tools like Alation or Collibra offer organizations the ability to document metadata, automate data classification, and provide user-friendly search interfaces to facilitate data access.

Data quality remains a central pillar of any governance initiative. High-quality data is essential for informed decision-making and reliable reporting. The integration of automated data quality tools allows healthcare organizations to monitor data accuracy, completeness, and consistency in real-time. Solutions such as Informatica Data Quality and Talend enable organizations to set parameters for acceptable data quality, automate cleansing processes, and generate reports that highlight any discrepancies. By embracing these technologies, healthcare providers ensure that decisions based on data are well-informed and grounded in accurate information.

Security and compliance are paramount within healthcare, making the role of technology in data governance even more critical. Regulatory frameworks such as HIPAA in the United States impose stringent requirements on how patient data should be handled, stored, and shared. Technologies such as data encryption, access controls, and audit trails have become indispensable tools in maintaining compliance. Solutions like Microsoft Azure Information Protection and IBM Security Guardium help organizations enforce encryption protocols, manage user access, and facilitate compliance audits. These tools create a secure ecosystem that not only protects patient data from breaches but also instills trust among patients, thereby supporting the overall objective of healthcare delivery.

In addition to security mechanisms, the adoption of artificial intelligence (AI) and machine learning (ML) enriches data governance by enhancing data analytics capabilities. AI-driven tools can sift through vast datasets, identifying patterns and insights that would otherwise remain untapped. These technologies enhance predictive analytics in clinical settings, facilitating risk assessments and population health management. For instance, platforms that utilize AI can streamline patient recruitment for clinical trials by analyzing patient data and identifying eligible candidates, thereby improving trial efficiency. Such applications underline the dual role of technology in fostering compliance while also enabling innovative healthcare solutions.

The integration of blockchain technology has emerged as a revolutionary approach to ensuring data integrity and security in healthcare. By providing a decentralized ledger system, blockchain enhances transparency and reduces the risk of data manipulation. Smart contracts can automate compliance processes, ensuring that stakeholder interactions are governed by predefined rules. This level of trust is essential in the healthcare landscape, where data sharing among various entities can often lead to concerns about data integrity and privacy. Blockchain-based solutions such as MedRec and Guardtime are pioneering applications that offer a secure framework for sharing patient data while adhering to regulations.

Moreover, the concept of data stewardship is gaining traction within healthcare organizations, emphasizing the importance of defining roles and responsibilities in managing data resources. Technology plays a vital role in supporting the governance structures that clarify these roles, ensuring accountability and ownership of data assets. Data stewardship tools, integrated with governance frameworks, empower organizations to delineate responsibilities related to data access, quality, and security. For example, tools like Apollo or Informatica's Enterprise Data Governance Suite foster collaboration among stakeholders, enabling a collective approach to data management.

For effective data governance, stakeholder engagement, and data literacy are essential. Collaborative tools enhance communication among governance teams, data custodians, and end-users. Solutions such as Microsoft Teams or Slack facilitate real-time discussions, fostering a culture of transparency and shared responsibility. Furthermore, technological training programs that emphasize the importance of data governance create a more informed workforce, allowing healthcare professionals to appreciate the implications of their data-related activities.

Yet, despite the myriad of available technologies, organizations must adopt a strategic approach when selecting tools for data governance. Alignment with organizational goals is crucial, as tools should not only address immediate needs but also be scalable and adaptable to future challenges. Evaluation criteria should include usability, interoperability with existing systems, and support for automation to minimize the manual effort associated with data governance tasks.

In conclusion, the intersection of technology and data governance in healthcare IT is fundamental for fostering a culture of compliance, security, and data quality. The ongoing evolution of tools—ranging from data catalogs to AI-driven analytics and blockchain—enables organizations to navigate the complexities of data governance effectively. By leveraging these technologies, healthcare organizations not only meet regulatory compliance demands but also unlock the potential for enhanced patient care, operational efficiency, and strategic decision-making. As healthcare continues to advance, the profound impact of innovative technologies on data governance will only grow, shaping the future of healthcare delivery.

8.1 Data Governance Software Solutions

The healthcare industry generates vast amounts of data daily, spanning clinical, operational, and financial domains. As organizations increasingly rely on this data for decision-making, patient care improvement, and regulatory compliance, the role of data governance has become critically important. Data governance encompasses the policies, processes, and responsibilities necessary for managing and protecting data assets throughout their lifecycle. To optimize these efforts, healthcare organizations are deploying data governance software solutions tailored to their unique needs.

At the heart of effective data governance lies the need for standardized frameworks that ensure data integrity, security, and compliance with regulations such as the Health Insurance Portability and Accountability Act (HIPAA) and the clinical trial regulations. Data governance software solutions equip organizations with the necessary tools to develop, enforce, and monitor governance policies, facilitating a culture of accountability and compliance.

One of the primary functions of data governance software is to enable data lineage tracking. Understanding the journey of data from its source to its destination is crucial in a healthcare environment, where the accuracy of patient records can have profound implications. With comprehensive data lineage capabilities, organizations can trace and visualize how data flows within their systems, revealing potential bottlenecks or vulnerabilities that could compromise data integrity. This transparency is vital for compliance audits and ensures that data can be trusted for clinical decision-making.

Another key aspect of these software solutions is their ability to facilitate data quality management. Poor data quality can lead to misinformed clinical decisions, increased operational costs, and damaged reputations. Advanced data governance software includes features that automate data profiling, cleansing, and enrichment processes. By identifying duplicates, inconsistencies, and inaccuracies in real time, organizations can maintain high-quality datasets that underpin effective decision-making and improve patient outcomes.

Identity and access management (IAM) are fundamental components of data governance in healthcare. Data governance software provides robust IAM features that enable organizations to implement role-based access controls, ensuring that only authorized personnel can access sensitive information. Effective IAM not only helps protect patient privacy but also simplifies compliance reporting and reduces the risk of data breaches—a critical concern in a sector where the implications of data misuse are severe.

Furthermore, effective data governance requires alignment between IT departments and clinical staff. This necessitates the creation of a data stewardship framework within healthcare organizations, ensuring that both technical and clinical perspectives inform governance strategies. Modern data governance software solutions often offer collaborative tools that promote cross-departmental communication, making it easier to establish a shared understanding of data responsibilities and priorities. These platforms enable data stewards to collaborate on data policies, monitor adherence, and address issues as they arise, thus fostering a data-driven culture.

Education and training are crucial for the success of any data governance initiative. Software solutions often incorporate training modules and resources that empower employees with the understanding and skills necessary to manage data effectively. Role-specific training ensures that all members of the organization, from board-level executives to clinical staff, understand their data governance responsibilities and the importance of data management practices. By embedding a culture of data governance within the organization, healthcare providers can create custodians of data who are invested in safeguarding data quality and integrity.

In addition to operational functions, healthcare data governance software also enhances data analytics capabilities. Equipped with data governance tools, organizations can establish a unified data ecosystem that allows for comprehensive insights across the enterprise. These analytics can be instrumental in identifying care gaps, analyzing patient outcomes, and driving research initiatives. By leveraging accurate and complete data, organizations can adopt strategies to enhance care delivery, optimize resource allocation, and ultimately elevate patient experiences.

Vendor selection plays a pivotal role in the successful implementation of data governance software solutions. Healthcare organizations must carefully assess the capabilities of different vendors, opting for those that align with their specific requirements, regulatory obligations, and long-term strategic objectives. Key considerations include ease of integration with existing systems, scalability, user-friendliness, and vendor support. Moreover, the chosen solution should be customizable to address the unique nuances of the organization's data governance needs.

Moreover, as healthcare providers increasingly migrate to cloud-based environments, data governance software solutions must be adaptable to various data storage models, whether on-premise, hybrid, or fully cloud-based. This adaptability ensures that governance practices can be enforced regardless of data location and enhances the visibility and traceability of data across different environments.

In conclusion, the intersection of healthcare IT and data governance is essential for ensuring the responsible management and protection of sensitive patient data. Data governance software solutions stand as critical enablers in this space, providing organizations with the tools to track data lineage, manage data quality, enforce access controls, and enhance collaboration. A commitment to robust data governance not only supports compliance and risk mitigation efforts but also positions healthcare organizations to leverage data as a strategic asset in improving patient outcomes and operational efficiency. As the healthcare landscape continues to evolve, the role of proficient data governance will undoubtedly grow, underscoring the necessity for innovative software solutions tailored to this critical domain.

8.2 Role of Artificial Intelligence and Machine Learning

The integration of artificial intelligence (AI) and machine learning (ML) into healthcare IT systems is revolutionizing various aspects of data governance. By enhancing data management, ensuring compliance with regulations, and improving decision-making capabilities, AI and ML provide robust frameworks for handling sensitive patient data while adhering to stringent privacy and security standards. Within this context, we explore the multifaceted roles these technologies play in optimizing data governance in the healthcare sector.

One of the paramount functions of AI and ML in healthcare data governance is data quality management. Accurate and reliable data is the cornerstone of effective healthcare delivery. AI algorithms can automatically assess data integrity by identifying anomalies, inconsistencies, and incomplete records. Machine learning models can learn from historical data patterns to flag potential errors and recommend corrective actions. This proactive approach not only streamlines data entry processes but also enhances the overall credibility of health records, fostering trust among healthcare professionals and patients alike.

Additionally, AI and ML significantly contribute to the realm of data compliance and risk assessment. The healthcare sector is governed by a plethora of regulations, including the Health Insurance Portability and Accountability Act (HIPAA) in the United States. Regulatory compliance necessitates robust data governance frameworks that can effectively monitor and manage access to patient information. Machine learning algorithms can analyze user behavior and identify deviations from typical access patterns, alerting data governance teams of potential breaches or compliance violations in real-time. By automating these risk assessments, healthcare organizations can respond swiftly to vulnerabilities, mitigating the risk of exposure and financial penalties while enhancing their overall security posture.

Moreover, the integration of AI and ML can lead to improved data accessibility without compromising security. In healthcare settings, timely access to data can be a matter of life and death. AI-powered solutions can facilitate secure data sharing among stakeholders—patients, providers, and payers—while ensuring that appropriate governance protocols are followed. For instance, natural language processing (NLP), a subset of AI, can help interpret unstructured data from electronic health records (EHRs) and make it more actionable. By enabling healthcare providers to gain insights from comprehensive datasets, these technologies support informed decision-making that enhances patient outcomes.

Incorporating AI and ML into healthcare data governance also helps address the increasing complexity posed by big data analytics. Healthcare organizations accumulate vast amounts of data from various sources, including wearables, imaging systems, and genomic data. The sheer volume and variety of this information can overwhelm traditional data management systems. Machine learning algorithms can derive meaningful insights from big data by automating the data preparation process, identifying trends, and generating predictive analytics. This data-driven approach empowers healthcare leaders to make strategic decisions based on empirical evidence rather than intuition, ultimately contributing to improved operational efficiencies.

Furthermore, machine learning has the potential to revolutionize patient privacy management in healthcare data governance. With growing concerns regarding data privacy breaches, organizations are under pressure to demonstrate compliance with privacy regulations. AI solutions can enable advanced privacy-preserving techniques, such as differential privacy, which allows organizations to glean insights from datasets without compromising individual patient identities. By anonymizing data while still permitting valuable analyses, healthcare organizations can explore population health trends while maintaining patient confidentiality.

The role of AI and ML extends to streamlining the overall data lifecycle management. Data governance involves the continuous management of data from creation to deletion. Machine learning algorithms can automate data classification and retention processes, categorizing data based on predefined governance policies. This automation facilitates regulatory compliance by ensuring that sensitive data is retained only as long as necessary, following the principles of data minimization and purpose limitation. As a result, healthcare organizations can reduce storage costs and enhance the efficiency of their data management practices.

In the pursuit of excellence in healthcare delivery, stakeholder engagement remains a critical element of data governance. AI and ML tools enhance communication between healthcare administrators, clinicians, and IT professionals by providing intuitive dashboards and visualizations of data governance metrics. These user-friendly interfaces enable stakeholders to collaborate more effectively and make shared decisions based on real-time data insights. As interdisciplinary teams work together to improve data governance, organizations can achieve their goals of quality care and operational efficiency.

The considerable strides made in AI and ML technologies are underscoring the importance of a proactive approach to healthcare data governance. Embracing these innovations yields a diverse range of benefits, including improved data quality, compliance, accessibility, and overall management efficiency. However, the advancement of AI and ML in data governance is not without challenges; organizations must remain vigilant about ethical considerations, bias mitigation, and transparency in algorithm design. Ultimately, the successful integration of these technologies will pave the way for a more secure and effective healthcare IT landscape, ensuring that patient care remains at the forefront while navigating the complexities of data governance.

8.3 Data Analytics and Reporting Tools

In the ever-evolving landscape of healthcare IT, data governance stands as an imperative pillar, ensuring that data integrity, security, and compliance are maintained. Increasingly, the integration of data analytics and reporting tools has become paramount to facilitate informed decision-making and enhance operational efficiencies within healthcare institutions. The application of these tools within the data governance framework allows organizations to derive valuable insights from their data, driving quality improvements and ensuring regulatory adherence.

Data analytics involves the systematic computational analysis of data sets to discover patterns, correlations, and trends. In healthcare, this involves the processing of vast volumes of data generated by electronic health records (EHRs), laboratory results, and patient management systems. Reporting tools complement analytics by visualizing this data, helping stakeholders understand complex information through dashboards, charts, and reports.

Effective data governance is underscored by three key principles: data accuracy, accessibility, and security. Advanced data analytics and reporting tools serve as enablers of these principles. For instance, implementing data quality analytics allows healthcare organizations to spot discrepancies and improve the accuracy of their data. Such analytics can identify missing data, incorrect entries, or duplicates, which can ultimately lead to better patient outcomes. Automated processes enable ongoing monitoring of data quality, which is vital for any organization seeking to uphold the standards mandated by regulatory bodies such as HIPAA and the CMS.

On the aspect of accessibility, data analytics tools facilitate the appropriate dissemination of information across the healthcare continuum. Healthcare professionals need real-time access to patient data to provide timely and safe care. Business Intelligence (BI) tools and self-service analytics platforms empower clinicians and administrative staff to extract and analyze data without requiring extensive technical expertise. This democratization of data ensures that clinical teams can make rapid decisions based on insights derived from comprehensive reports and dashboards, leading to improved patient care and operational excellence.

The importance of data security cannot be overstated in the context of healthcare IT. With the pervasive threat of data breaches and increasing regulatory scrutiny, specialized analytics tools aid in monitoring data access, identifying anomalies, and ensuring compliance with security policies. Tools designed for robust data governance often incorporate features for auditing and tracking data usage, which can help healthcare organizations meet the requirements of healthcare regulations more effectively. Through predictive analytics, organizations can anticipate potential security threats, thereby enhancing their proactive measures to safeguard sensitive patient data.

Another compelling dimension of data analytics within healthcare is its capacity for population health management. By aggregating and analyzing data from diverse sources—such as EHRs, social determinants of health, and patient-generated data—healthcare organizations can identify population trends and health disparities. Predictive analytics can be used to forecast disease outbreaks, manage chronic conditions, and reduce hospital readmission rates. By leveraging these insights, targeted interventions can be devised, ultimately fostering better health outcomes and a more efficient allocation of resources.

Moreover, reporting tools allow organizations to visualize data in ways that convey complex healthcare metrics clearly and succinctly. This capability is crucial for stakeholders, ranging from healthcare executives to clinical staff, as it aids in the interpretation of key performance indicators (KPIs). For example, dashboard tools can provide real-time insights into clinical workflows, patient throughput, and operational metrics. These visual aids enhance strategic decision-making, allowing organizations to pivot and adapt in response to changing healthcare dynamics.

The integration of machine learning (ML) and artificial intelligence (AI) into data analytics further augments the capabilities of healthcare IT systems. These technologies can deepen insights derived from data and provide recommendations based on historical patterns. For instance, ML algorithms can identify risk factors for specific patient populations, allowing for preventative measures that ultimately reduce costs and enhance care. The resulting insights can be reported in accessible formats, aiding healthcare providers in understanding complex patient data and tailoring their care strategies accordingly.

However, the successful implementation of data analytics and reporting tools requires a well-defined data governance strategy. Organizations must cultivate a culture of data stewardship where stakeholders understand the significance of data integrity and adhere to governance policies. Training sessions, ongoing support, and clear communication regarding data ownership responsibilities strengthen the framework needed for optimal utilization of analytics.

Furthermore, organizations should prioritize interoperability and data exchange among different systems. Data analytics tools are most effective when they can aggregate data from diverse sources. Standards such as Fast Healthcare Interoperability Resources (FHIR) can facilitate seamless data sharing, empowering analytics tools to provide comprehensive insights across various platforms.

In conclusion, the role of data analytics and reporting tools in healthcare IT is transformative, particularly within the scope of data governance. By enabling accurate data management, enhancing accessibility, ensuring security, and informing decision-making, these tools contribute to the overarching goal of delivering high-quality patient care while adhering to regulatory requirements. As healthcare moves towards a more data-driven future, the integration of advanced analytics and robust reporting mechanisms will be critical in navigating the challenges and opportunities that lie ahead. Embracing these technologies is not merely a tactical maneuver; it is a strategic imperative for healthcare organizations committed to excellence in data governance.

Chapter 9: Case Studies and Best Practices

Data governance in healthcare IT is a critical discourse that shapes the quality of patient care, operational efficiency, and regulatory compliance. In an era where healthcare organizations grapple with vast amounts of data generated each day, establishing robust data governance frameworks through case studies and best practices provides insightful pathways for effective data management. Understanding the nuance of these frameworks is essential for organizations aiming to optimize their workflow while ensuring the integrity and security of patient data.

One exemplary case study of successful data governance is the implementation at Kaiser Permanente, one of the largest integrated healthcare systems in the United States. Kaiser Permanente has developed a comprehensive data governance structure that involves the coordination of various stakeholders across the organization. Central to their approach is the establishment of a Data Governance Council tasked with overseeing the policies and procedures governing data management. This council comprises representatives from various departments, including IT, clinical operations, and compliance, fostering a holistic view of data across the organization.

Key to their success has been the commitment to developing standardized data definitions and metadata management. By creating a common vocabulary for data elements used within their EHR system, the organization ensures consistency and clarity. This harmonization enables not just effective communication, but also facilitates interdepartmental collaboration and data sharing. The systematic approach taken by Kaiser Permanente serves as a benchmark for other healthcare organizations striving for similar coherence in their data governance efforts.

Another notable example can be found at the University of California Health (UCH), which has embraced data governance as a strategic initiative to improve data quality, accessibility, and compliance with regulatory standards. UCH engaged in a thorough assessment of current data practices and developed an expansive data governance framework focusing on accountability, transparency, and data stewardship. Through the formation of data stewards within each department, accountability for data integrity was heightened. These stewards serve as liaisons between governance bodies and functional areas, ensuring that data management practices are adhered to at every level.

The introduction of advanced analytics has compelled UCH to rethink data governance further. By leveraging predictive analytics and artificial intelligence, they support clinical decisions and enhance patient outcomes. This advancement necessitated not just a governance model, but a robust data architecture that accommodates the scale and intricacy of modern data uses. UCH successfully demonstrates the vital role that data governance plays in enhancing the efficacy of data analytics, ultimately fostering evidence-based healthcare delivery.

Best practices derived from these cases highlight the necessity of developing a clear governance framework that prioritizes data quality, security, and compliance. Organizations must define explicit roles and responsibilities for data governance, ensuring that all stakeholders are aligned with the strategic goals of the organization. Moreover, continuous training and education on data governance principles for all staff are crucial to cultivate a culture of data stewardship.

Moreover, integrating data governance into everyday operational workflows is vital. Rather than treating governance as a separate entity, it should be woven into the fabric of routine processes. This can be achieved by embedding governance practices into technology solutions, such as EHR systems, to facilitate real-time monitoring of data quality and access controls.

Another significant best practice is the reliance on technology to enforce governance policies. Healthcare organizations ought to utilize tools for data cataloging, lineage tracking, and metadata management. By implementing these technologies, organizations can gain greater visibility into their data assets and ensure compliance with applicable regulations such as HIPAA and GDPR. This technological backing complements the human aspect of governance, creating a more resilient framework.

Collaboration across departments is also a fundamental practice in effective data governance. The separation of data governance from operational workflows can lead to silos that inhibit the potential of data. Encouraging interdisciplinary teams that include clinical, administrative, and IT professionals allows for comprehensive input into governance decisions. This collaborative approach enhances data sharing and fosters innovation, resulting in improved patient care and operational efficiency.

Furthermore, regular audit and evaluation of data governance measures should be integral to any governance framework. Continuous assessment enables organizations to identify gaps in compliance, data quality, and overall efficiencies. Utilizing performance metrics tied to data governance objectives can provide valuable insights that inform decision-making processes and guide adjustments to governance policies.

The evolving landscape of healthcare IT necessitates agility in data governance. Emerging trends, such as telehealth and personalized medicine, introduce new data challenges that must be addressed through diligent governance. Organizations that remain vigilant and responsive to such developments will not only enhance their data management capabilities but also achieve a competitive edge in the healthcare sector.

In conclusion, the case studies illustrated by Kaiser Permanente and the University of California Health provide valuable lessons in the importance of establishing effective data governance frameworks. By adopting best practices that emphasize collaboration, technology integration, and ongoing evaluation, healthcare organizations can optimize their data governance initiatives. Such efforts not only bolster the integrity and security of patient data but also cultivate a culture of accountability and continuous improvement within the healthcare ecosystem. As the industry continues to evolve, the imperative for robust data governance will only grow, making it an indispensable component of successful healthcare IT management.

9.1 Successful Data Governance Models in Healthcare

Data governance has emerged as a crucial element within the healthcare sector, especially given the complexity and sensitivity of data involved. In an era where digital health records, telemedicine, and personalized medicine are becoming the norm, effective data governance models are essential for enhancing patient care, ensuring compliance with regulations, and maintaining data integrity. Successful models often share key characteristics that set them apart from traditional governance frameworks.

A foundational aspect of successful data governance in healthcare is stakeholder engagement. This engagement must extend beyond IT leadership to encompass clinical practitioners, administrators, compliance officers, and even patients. Diverse stakeholder involvement fosters collective ownership and responsibility for data stewardship, resulting in enhanced data quality and trustworthiness. For instance, organizations that include clinicians in data governance discussions can better understand direct implications on patient care and can formulate guidelines that simplify rather than complicate healthcare workflows.

Another hallmark of effective data governance is the establishment of clear roles and responsibilities. Successful models delineate who is accountable for data accuracy, security, and accessibility. This involves appointing data stewards across various departments, each responsible for specific datasets. In a well-defined governance framework, data stewards work collaboratively and ensure adherence to standards and policies. They act as liaisons between data users

138

and technical teams, facilitating better communication and data integrity. This model empowers individuals who are closest to the data to take charge of its management, which can lead to improved outcomes and a culture of accountability.

The integration of technology into data governance practices is also critical. Healthcare organizations utilizing advanced analytics, machine learning, and artificial intelligence can benefit from smarter data management strategies. For example, through automated data lineage tracking, organizations can better understand the flow of data, ensuring that data governance rules are consistently applied. Moreover, AI-driven tools can be employed to flag anomalies in data reporting, thus providing a proactive means to manage data quality. By leveraging technological capabilities, healthcare organizations can promote data stewardship at scale, which aligns well with the pressing demands of population health management.

Successful data governance models are characterized by the establishment and enforcement of standardized policies and procedures. These policies not only define acceptable data usage but also outline protocols for data access and sharing. Compliance with regulations such as HIPAA necessitates robust strategies for securing patient information while ensuring it is available for necessary medical insights. Regular training and awareness programs targeted at all staff levels can be beneficial in embedding these practices into the organizational culture. Clear documentation and transparency in data governance efforts can also facilitate audits and demonstrate compliance, building trust with regulatory bodies and patients alike.

Furthermore, data governance initiatives are often more successful when they incorporate a continuous improvement mechanism. By employing techniques such as performance measurement and benchmarking, organizations can assess the effectiveness of their data governance strategies and pivot when necessary. Feedback loops enable healthcare institutions to gain insights into ongoing challenges in data quality or compliance issues, leading to timely interventions. For example, regular stakeholder surveys can pinpoint areas of misalignment between data governance policies and operational realities, paving the way for targeted enhancements.

Interoperability is another critical success factor in data governance models within healthcare. The ability to share and utilize data across disparate systems and institutions is essential for holistic patient care. Successful models prioritize the adoption of standards that facilitate seamless data exchange. Emphasis on interoperability ensures that data governance policies do not hinder the free flow of data but rather enhance its utility. Such models enable healthcare providers to synthesize information from various platforms, informing clinical decision-making and improving patient outcomes.

Lastly, many successful data governance frameworks incorporate patient-centered approaches. Involving patients as data partners is becoming increasingly important as healthcare recognizes the value of patient-generated data. By empowering patients with control over their health data—via consent protocols and transparency mechanisms—healthcare organizations can foster a collaborative environment. This not only boosts patient engagement but also aligns data governance practices with ethical standards of care.

In conclusion, healthcare organizations aiming to enhance their data governance initiatives must focus on stakeholder engagement, clear role definitions, the integration of technology, standardized policies, continuous improvement, interoperability, and patient-centered approaches. Employing these strategies will not only facilitate compliance and security but will also enhance the overall quality of care delivered to patients. As the healthcare landscape continues to evolve, the integration of robust data governance models will remain a linchpin in achieving both operational excellence and positive patient experiences. The future of healthcare data governance hinges on these successful frameworks, driving the continual advancement of healthcare delivery in an increasingly data-rich environment.

9.2 Lessons Learned from Failures

In healthcare IT, data governance is a critical framework that ensures the accuracy, availability, and security of health information. However, despite its significance, healthcare organizations often encounter failures in implementing effective data governance. These failures not only disrupt operations but also jeopardize patient care and organizational integrity. Analyzing these setbacks reveals nine vital lessons that can inform better practices and enhance data governance frameworks in healthcare.

Firstly, establishing clear ownership and accountability is imperative. Many organizations suffer due to a lack of defined roles when it comes to data governance. Without clear assignments, data stewardship becomes muddled, leading to compromised decision-making and eventual failures in compliance. Designated data owners must be identified across departments, ensuring responsibility is shared and reinforced. This clarity enables swift responses to data issues, accountability extends to every stakeholder, and the overall reliability of data management improves.

Secondly, regular communication is essential. In healthcare settings, data governance often intersects with various clinical, financial, and operational stakeholders. Ineffective communication can result in inconsistencies and misunderstandings regarding data policies and practices. Implementing a structured communication plan, including periodic meetings, updates, and forums for feedback, fosters collaboration. This lesson underscores that successful data governance is not solely about technology—it's a cooperative endeavor that thrives on strong interpersonal connections.

Thirdly, investing in data governance training and education is key. Many healthcare IT failures stem from a lack of understanding of data governance policies among staff. Organizations often neglect to provide adequate training programs, leading to non-compliance and errors in data management practices. By proactively promoting a culture of continuous learning, organizations can ensure that employees are well-versed in best practices, regulations, and their specific roles within the governance framework. This investment serves as a protective measure against future failures.

Fourthly, integrating data governance into organizational strategy is vital. Data governance initiatives should not exist in a vacuum; they must be aligned with the broader objectives of the organization. A failure to weave governance considerations into strategic planning can result in initiatives that lack organizational buy-in and resources. When governance is positioned as a fundamental component of the organizational mission, it engenders a sense of ownership at all levels and creates an environment where data governance is viewed as an enabler of success rather than merely a regulatory requirement.

Fifthly, implementing tools and technologies that facilitate data governance is crucial. Many organizations still rely on outdated systems that cannot handle the complexities of modern data management. Failures typically arise from the inability to track data lineage, ensure data quality, or comply with regulatory requirements. Embracing advanced tools—such as data cataloging, data quality management software, and audit trails—can significantly enhance data governance capabilities. Organizations must periodically evaluate their technology stack to ensure it evolves alongside their data needs.

Sixthly, prioritizing data quality cannot be overemphasized. Poor data quality underpins many failures in data governance frameworks. Inaccuracies in health records, duplicates, and incomplete datasets can lead to erroneous clinical decisions and regulatory infractions. A relentless focus on data quality—through metrics, audits, and cleansing processes—can mitigate these issues. Organizations must adopt a mindset that views data quality as a continuous journey rather than a one-time initiative, thereby embedding it into the organization's culture.

Seventhly, stakeholder engagement is paramount for sustainable governance. Data governance ultimately affects various stakeholders, including clinicians, administrators, and patients. Implementing a governance framework without considering these stakeholders' needs and perspectives leads to resistance and ineffective policies. Engaging stakeholders in the development of governance models not only enhances compliance but also promotes a sense of ownership. It establishes a collaborative approach to governance, making policies relevant and actionable across the board.

Eighthly, adaptability in data governance practices is essential. The rapid pace of change in healthcare technology and regulations demands a flexible governance approach. Many organizations fail when they rigidly adhere to outdated frameworks that do not accommodate emerging trends such as artificial intelligence, telehealth, or personalized medicine. An adaptable governance framework acknowledges the evolving landscape of healthcare IT and incorporates feedback loops for continuous improvement. Organizations should regularly assess and iterate their governance practices to remain agile and responsive to change.

Lastly, measuring success through key performance indicators (KPIs) is fundamental. Many organizations overlook the importance of quantifiable metrics to assess the effectiveness of their data governance practices. Without a systematic approach to evaluate progress, it becomes challenging to identify weaknesses or areas for improvement. Establishing clear KPIs related to compliance, data quality, and stakeholder satisfaction allows organizations to monitor their governance efforts, ensuring accountability and facilitating iterative enhancements over time.

In conclusion, the complexities of data governance in healthcare IT necessitate a multifaceted approach to mitigate failures and enhance outcomes. By embracing these lessons learned from past missteps, healthcare organizations can forge more robust governance frameworks that protect patient information, foster compliance, and ultimately contribute to improved patient care. Implementing strategic ownership, enhancing communication, prioritizing education and quality, and embracing adaptability equips healthcare organizations to navigate the intricate landscape of modern data governance confidently.

9.3 Future Trends in Data Governance

In the rapidly evolving landscape of healthcare IT, data governance stands as a critical pillar for ensuring the integrity, security, and accessibility of health data. With the confluence of advanced technologies and emerging regulatory frameworks, the future of data governance in healthcare will be defined by several pivotal trends that not only address existing challenges but also anticipate future needs of healthcare organizations and their stakeholders.

One of the most significant trends is the increasing emphasis on data interoperability. The ability to exchange health information seamlessly across different systems is paramount for improving patient outcomes and enhancing care coordination. Regulatory bodies like the Office of the National Coordinator for Health Information Technology (ONC) have set forth standards aimed at facilitating interoperability. As these regulations evolve, data governance frameworks will need to adapt by incorporating protocols for data sharing, usage policies, and real-time data access. This transformation will push organizations to rethink their governance strategies, focusing on collaborative data ecosystems that break down silos across disparate healthcare entities.

Moreover, the advent of advanced analytics and artificial intelligence (AI) is reshaping the governance landscape. Healthcare organizations are increasingly leveraging AI to analyze vast datasets for predictive modeling, clinical decision-making, and operational optimization. As these technologies gain traction, there will be a growing need for robust data governance frameworks that ensure ethical use of AI and accountability in automated processes. This includes defining data provenance, ensuring data quality, and providing

146

transparency in AI-driven insights. As AI systems become more autonomous, governance frameworks must evolve to address risks associated with bias, privacy, and algorithmic transparency.

Privacy issues are also paramount in shaping the future of data governance in healthcare IT. The increasing sophistication of cyber threats necessitates an evolution of data protection strategies. Healthcare organizations face a dual challenge: adhering to stringent regulations such as the Health Insurance Portability and Accountability Act (HIPAA) while simultaneously safeguarding against cyber vulnerabilities. The future will see a shift towards a proactive approach to data governance, integrating cybersecurity measures directly into governance policies. This includes implementing continual risk assessments, incident response protocols, and employee training programs focused on cyber hygiene. Increasing reliance on cloud services and third-party vendors will further necessitate rigorous governance checks to ensure compliance and data integrity.

Data stewardship will become increasingly centralized to enhance data quality and integrity. As organizations generate and consume more health data, a comprehensive stewardship model will be required. This model would encompass Data Steward roles focused on overseeing data quality, lineage, and access controls. By establishing clear responsibilities and accountability for data management, healthcare IT systems can improve overall data trustworthiness. Enhanced stewardship can lead to better decision-making, as stakeholders can rely on accurate and comprehensive data to guide their clinical and operational strategies.

As social determinants of health (SDOH) gain traction, data governance will increasingly extend beyond clinical data to incorporate a wide array of information types. Factors such as socioeconomic status, housing instability, and access to transportation must be considered to provide holistic patient care. The future will see healthcare organizations adopting more nuanced data governance frameworks that support the integration of SDOH data into their analytics streams. This will require new policies around data collection, confidentiality, and consent management. By prioritizing SDOH within data governance, stakeholders can foster a more equitable healthcare landscape, ultimately leading to better health outcomes for diverse populations.

In light of the increasing complexity of healthcare data management, there will also be a growing focus on training and development of personnel involved in data governance. The demand for skilled professionals who understand both healthcare landscape intricacies and data governance principles is on the rise. Educational initiatives will be paramount to ensure that staff across the healthcare spectrum are well-versed in data governance protocols and practices. Professional organizations will likely spearhead these initiatives, developing certification programs and best practice frameworks geared specifically towards healthcare data governance.

Regulatory compliance will remain a cornerstone of data governance in healthcare IT. As government oversight expands, healthcare organizations must stay abreast of changing regulations at both the federal and state levels. This necessitates an agile governance framework capable of adapting to new compliance mandates without compromising data integrity or security efforts. Organizations must invest in technology solutions that enable real-time compliance monitoring and reporting, thereby reducing the burden of manual oversight. The proactive management of compliance requirements will position organizations to swiftly address regulatory changes while mitigating risks associated with noncompliance.

Finally, as healthcare becomes increasingly consumer-centric, patient engagement in their own healthcare data governance will rise. Patients will demand greater transparency and control over their health information, requiring healthcare organizations to redefine their engagement strategies. This collaborative approach to governance will prompt the development of user-friendly platforms that empower patients to manage their data, understand their rights, and even participate in data-sharing decisions. In embracing patient-driven governance, healthcare organizations not only enhance trust but also leverage patient insights to drive better healthcare delivery.

In conclusion, the future of data governance in healthcare IT is on the cusp of transformative change. From enhanced interoperability and AI accountability to the integration of socioeconomic factors and patient engagement, the trends shaping this landscape will be profound. Forward-thinking organizations that invest in robust governance frameworks, agile compliance strategies, skilled personnel, and patient empowerment will be positioned not merely to adapt, but to thrive in the increasingly complex world of healthcare data management.

Chapter 10: Conclusion and Future Directions

The domain of data governance in healthcare IT is at a pivotal juncture, driven by rapid technological advancements and increasing regulatory scrutiny. As healthcare organizations streamline operations and harness the power of data analytics, the importance of robust data governance frameworks becomes increasingly evident. The culmination of this discourse, encapsulated in the analysis and insights gathered throughout this exploration, reveals both the accomplishments and challenges that lie ahead in data governance within healthcare IT.

The successes in data governance largely stem from the realization of data as a critical asset. Organizations are increasingly principled in their approach, understanding that well-governed data enhances patient care, operational efficiencies, and regulatory compliance. Comprehensive frameworks that articulate roles, responsibilities, and policies surrounding data handling have been integrated into organizational cultures. The establishment of data governance committees, incorporating interdisciplinary stakeholders ranging from IT professionals to healthcare providers, underscores a shift towards collaborative management of data assets.

Moreover, the introduction of technologies such as artificial intelligence (AI) and machine learning (ML) has ushered in a new era of data utilization. These tools rely heavily on high-quality, well-governed data to produce meaningful insights and support clinical decision-making. The synergy between AI-driven applications and effective data governance practices has been recognized as a catalyst for enhancing patient outcomes and operational resilience. However, this synthesis also necessitates sophisticated governance strategies to ensure transparency, accountability, and compliance with ethical standards. As AI systems evolve, the frameworks surrounding them must adapt to address the complexities they introduce.

Regulatory requirements further complicate the landscape. Evolving legislation, such as the Health Insurance Portability and Accountability Act (HIPAA) and the 21st Century Cures Act, mandates healthcare organizations to safeguard patient data diligently. Compliance with these regulations is not only a legal obligation but also a moral imperative, establishing trust between patients and healthcare providers. Organizations that effectively integrate regulatory requirements into their data governance strategies not only mitigate risks but also position themselves as leaders in patient data protection.

However, while progress has been made, substantial barriers to effective data governance persist. Fragmented data sources across various platforms can exacerbate discrepancies and lead to inaccurate reporting. This fragmentation underscores the necessity for interoperability—a critical yet challenging aspect of healthcare IT. Data silos inhibit the seamless flow of information, rendering comprehensive data governance efforts ineffective. Future directions must emphasize the development and adoption of standardized data formats and protocols to foster interoperability across healthcare systems.

Additionally, healthcare organizations often grapple with the cultural shifts required for effective data governance. Resistance from staff and stakeholders accustomed to traditional workflows can hinder the implementation of new policies and procedures. Thus, cultivating a culture that recognizes and prioritizes data governance is essential. This entails ongoing education, training, and engagement strategies to inform stakeholders about the value of data governance in enhancing patient care and organizational performance.

The emphasis on data ethics and privacy cannot be overstated in this discussion. With data breaches becoming more prevalent, healthcare organizations must prioritize ethical considerations in their governance strategies. The increasing reliance on personal health information raises concerns over data security and individual privacy. Adopting ethical data governance frameworks that address these concerns will not only safeguard against data misuse but also reinforce patient confidence in healthcare institutions.

Emerging technologies, particularly blockchain, present exciting opportunities for enhancing data governance in healthcare IT. Blockchain's inherent characteristics of decentralization, transparency, and security offer innovative pathways for improving data integrity and sharing. By leveraging blockchain, healthcare organizations can facilitate secure data exchanges while ensuring that patient consent is both captured and honored. Future research and experimentation with this technology could revolutionize existing governance models, potentially leading to a more secure and interoperable healthcare ecosystem.

As the landscape of healthcare IT continues to evolve, the role of data governance will expand, necessitating adaptability and foresight from healthcare organizations. Strategic planning focused on scalability, future-proofing governance structures, and maintaining adaptability in the face of technological changes will be essential. This includes a proactive approach to emerging trends and technologies, as well as a flexible mindset that embraces continuous learning and improvement.

Moreover, collaboration between healthcare organizations, technology vendors, regulatory bodies, and academic institutions will be paramount to address common challenges in data governance. Establishing partnerships to share best practices, fostering innovation, and advocating for policy changes that support effective governance will promote a more unified approach to managing health data.

In conclusion, the evolution of data governance in healthcare IT signifies a transformative journey marked by both achievements and challenges. While significant strides have been made, the road ahead requires a commitment to refining frameworks, addressing interoperability, fostering a culture of governance, upholding data ethics, and embracing innovative technologies. By intensifying efforts in these domains, healthcare organizations can harness the full potential of data, ultimately leading to enhanced patient care, operational efficiencies, and a more resilient healthcare system. By envisioning a future rooted in robust data governance, the healthcare sector can ensure that it remains aligned with the evolving landscape of patient needs, technological advancements, and regulatory expectations.

10.1 Summary of Key Takeaways

Data governance in healthcare IT is paramount for ensuring the integrity, security, and optimal use of information within the vast and complex healthcare landscape. As the healthcare industry continues to transform with technological advancements, a robust framework for data governance becomes increasingly essential. Below are ten key takeaways that encapsulate the pivotal aspects of data governance in this sector.

Firstly, the foundational principle of data governance in healthcare IT is the establishment of clear ownership and accountability. Identifying data stewards—individuals or teams responsible for managing specific data sets—ensures that there is a designated authority to uphold data quality and compliance. This accountability is not merely bureaucratic; it is critical for improving data accuracy and reliability, which in turn informs clinical decisions and operational management.

Secondly, regulatory compliance is a cornerstone of data governance. As healthcare organizations navigate a myriad of regulations, including the Health Insurance Portability and Accountability Act (HIPAA), it is crucial to implement governance frameworks that ensure compliance with federal, state, and local laws. Regular audits and assessments should be integrated into the governance strategy to identify potential compliance risks and rectify them proactively.

Thirdly, data quality management is an integral component of effective data governance. The principle of 'garbage in, garbage out' aptly illustrates the consequences of poor data quality in healthcare settings. Data inaccuracies can lead to misguided clinical decisions, faulty billing practices, and failed population health initiatives. Establishing rigorous protocols for data entry, validation, and ongoing monitoring can mitigate these risks and promote a culture of quality.

Fourth, stakeholder engagement is vital for a successful data governance framework. In contrast to a top-down approach, involving a diverse range of stakeholders—including clinical staff, IT professionals, compliance officers, and executive leadership—ensures that the governance policies align with actual operational needs and challenges. This collaborative approach fosters a shared understanding of the importance of data governance across the organization, enhancing buy-in and support.

Fifth, the use of standardized data definitions and classification systems facilitates interoperability and improves data sharing across different systems and entities. Establishing a common language for data elements ensures that information is consistently captured and interpreted, reducing discrepancies and enhancing the continuity of care. For healthcare IT, adopting widely accepted standards such as Fast Healthcare Interoperability Resources (FHIR) is essential for effective data exchange.

Sixth, healthcare organizations must recognize the importance of data security in governance frameworks. The sensitive nature of healthcare data necessitates stringent security measures to protect against breaches, unauthorized access, and data loss. Implementing advanced security technologies, conducting regular risk assessments, and fostering a culture of cybersecurity awareness are crucial actions that must be taken to secure health information.

Seventh, longitudinal health data tracking is an increasingly vital aspect of data governance. With the rise of value-based care models, healthcare stakeholders must be able to track patient data over time. Establishing structures to aggregate and analyze longitudinal data can provide insights into patient outcomes, treatment effectiveness, and overall population health trends. This capability supports informed decision-making at both the individual and organizational levels.

Eighth, educating the workforce about data governance principles and practices is imperative for success. Continuous training and awareness initiatives equip healthcare staff with the knowledge necessary to understand the implications of data governance, address data handling best practices, and foster a culture of data stewardship. A well-informed workforce will enable organizations to leverage data more effectively while minimizing risks.

Ninth, the role of technology cannot be overstated in the context of data governance. Advanced analytics, artificial intelligence, and machine learning can significantly enhance data governance efforts by automating data quality checks, enabling sophisticated data stewardship processes, and providing predictive insights. Embracing these technologies allows healthcare organizations to streamline their data governance efforts and improve overall data utility.

Finally, a dynamic, adaptive approach to data governance is crucial in today's rapidly evolving healthcare landscape. The emergence of new technologies, evolving regulations, and shifting industry standards necessitate flexible governance frameworks that can adapt to change without compromising on integrity or compliance. Organizations should establish feedback mechanisms to assess and refine their governance strategies continually, ensuring they remain relevant and effective in addressing emerging challenges.

In conclusion, the efficacy of data governance in healthcare IT is fundamental to achieving the industry's operational and clinical goals. By establishing clear accountability structures, ensuring compliance, maintaining data quality, engaging stakeholders, implementing security measures, and leveraging technology, healthcare organizations can develop a robust framework for data governance. As the healthcare landscape evolves, the principles outlined above provide a comprehensive roadmap for navigating the complexities of data governance and ultimately driving better health outcomes.

10.2 The Evolving Role of Data Governance

Data governance in healthcare IT has evolved into a critical pillar for organizations navigating the complexities of managing vast amounts of sensitive patient information. As digital health technologies proliferate, the need for robust governance frameworks that ensure data integrity, privacy, security, and compliance has become imperative. In this landscape, data governance is not merely about policies and procedures; it encompasses a holistic approach involving people, processes, and technologies that collectively influence how healthcare data is handled across its lifecycle.

At the forefront of this evolution is the increasing recognition of data as a strategic asset. Historically, healthcare organizations often viewed data through a transactional lens—essentially as a byproduct of operations. However, with the rise of data analytics, clinical decision support systems, and predictive modeling, data has transformed into a vital resource capable of driving insights and improving health outcomes. This paradigm shift necessitates the establishment of comprehensive governance structures to maximize data utility while minimizing risks associated with its misuse.

In the realm of data governance, transparency has emerged as a fundamental principle. Stakeholders, including patients, practitioners, and regulatory bodies expect clarity in data handling practices. Initiatives aimed at enhancing transparency involve creating clear communication channels and frameworks that elucidate data collection methodologies, usage policies, and access controls. Patients increasingly demand to know how their data is utilized and shared, propelling healthcare organizations to adopt practices that not only comply with regulations like HIPAA but also align with patient expectations for privacy and autonomy.

The integration of artificial intelligence (AI) and machine learning (ML) into healthcare systems further complicates data governance. These technologies have the potential to transform patient care by providing actionable insights from vast datasets. However, their effectiveness hinges on the quality of the underlying data and the governance in place to manage it. To harness the power of AI and ML, healthcare organizations must prioritize data accuracy, standardization, and contextual understanding. Governance frameworks must evolve to incorporate best practices for data hygiene, ensuring that the algorithms developed are not only efficient but also ethical and free from biases that can exacerbate health disparities.

Moreover, regulatory compliance continues to be a pivotal aspect of data governance. The rapid technological advancement within healthcare has led to a mosaic of regulations at local, national, and international levels. Organizations must not only comply with existing frameworks but also remain agile to adapt to new legislation. Failure to navigate the intricacies of regulations can result in severe penalties and loss of patient trust. Consequently, a proactive approach to governance includes establishing compliance protocols and engaging in continuous education and training for staff regarding data regulations, security practices, and ethical considerations.

Cross-functional governance is another critical trend in the sector. Traditionally, data governance initiatives may have been siloed within IT departments or compliance teams. However, the evolving nature of healthcare requires collaboration across clinical, operational, and technological domains. Effective governance hinges on the alignment of diverse stakeholders' interests, including clinicians, data scientists, and administrative personnel. This integrated approach ensures that governance policies reflect the practical realities of data usage while fostering a culture of accountability and shared ownership.

Emerging technologies, such as blockchain, are also poised to influence data governance frameworks within healthcare. By providing secure, verifiable, and immutable records of transactions, blockchain technology can enhance data integrity and facilitate more transparent data-sharing agreements between entities. Such technological advancements necessitate that governance protocols are adaptable and forward-looking, capable of facilitating innovation while safeguarding data integrity and patient privacy.

The focus on patient-centric governance is another significant evolution. As patients assume a more active role in their healthcare journeys, organizations must reevaluate their governance strategies to align with this shift. Empowering patients with greater control over their data not only fosters trust but also enhances data quality through patient engagement in reporting their health status and experiences. Developing strategies that prioritize patient involvement in data governance can lead to more personalized care models, thus improving health outcomes.

Lastly, the increasing importance of data ethics in governance frameworks cannot be overlooked. The capability to collect and analyze vast amounts of data introduces ethical dilemmas regarding consent, bias, and data stewardship. Organizations must consider the moral implications of their data governance practices, ensuring they uphold the principles of fairness and equity in their implementation. This ethical lens encourages healthcare entities to assess not just what can be done with data, but what should be done—an essential consideration in promoting social justice in healthcare delivery.

In summary, the role of data governance within healthcare IT is undergoing a transformative evolution. It requires a multifaceted approach that integrates transparency, collaboration, compliance, technological innovation, patient engagement, and ethical considerations. As healthcare organizations continue to grapple with the implications of their data governance practices, they must remain vigilant, adaptable, and responsive to the dynamic landscape of healthcare information management. By embracing these tenets, organizations can not only mitigate risks but also leverage data governance as a catalyst for innovation and improved patient care.

10.3 Recommendations for Healthcare Organizations

Effective data governance is pivotal in shaping the landscape of healthcare IT. The intricate interplay between technology, patient care, and regulatory compliance necessitates a robust framework that ensures data integrity, security, and privacy. To navigate the complexities of regulating sensitive health information while enhancing patient outcomes, healthcare organizations must adopt multiple strategies focusing on data governance. Here are ten recommendations that can inform their approach.

First, establishing a dedicated data governance committee is essential. This multidisciplinary team should encompass stakeholders from IT, compliance, legal, clinical operations, and management. The committee's responsibility is to craft a clear data governance strategy aligned with organizational objectives. By engaging varied expertise, the committee can ensure that diverse perspectives contribute to data stewardship policies and facilitate a holistic view of data usage across departments.

Second, organizations should invest in comprehensive data governance training programs for all employees. Understanding the importance of data governance is fundamental for all staff, as they play crucial roles in handling patient information, often without knowing the implications of their actions. Effective education fosters a culture of accountability and emphasizes adherence to policies, thereby minimizing risks associated with data breaches or mismanagement.

Third, organizations must implement robust data quality management processes. Data integrity is paramount to informed decision-making in healthcare. Establishing standardized protocols for data entry, regular audits for data accuracy, and rectification procedures can significantly enhance the quality of health records. Organizations should utilize technology-driven solutions, such as automated validation tools, to maintain a high level of data consistency across all systems.

Fourth, a clear data classification framework should be developed. Identifying and categorizing data based on its sensitivity and value is crucial for effective governance. By classifying data, organizations can enforce appropriate access controls and data handling practices, ensuring that sensitive patient information is managed according to regulations like HIPAA, while promoting data sharing and interoperability where appropriate.

Fifth, healthcare organizations need to establish a data stewardship model. Designating data stewards within departments enhances accountability for data use. Stewards should be responsible for ensuring data compliance, training team members on best practices, and acting as liaisons between clinical staff and IT. This direct line of communication helps to bridge gaps in understanding the technicalities of data usage while highlighting functional needs and challenges.

Sixth, organizations should prioritize the integration of data governance with existing IT frameworks. Seamlessly incorporating data governance into technology infrastructures ensures that governance guidelines are enforced across the board. Implementing tools such as data catalogs and lineage tracking can empower organizations to trace data flows, understand its origin, and assess interoperability across systems while ensuring that all data management processes remain compliant.

Seventh, organizations must embrace robust data security protocols. As cybersecurity threats proliferate, organizations must prioritize safeguarding sensitive patient information. This includes implementing strong encryption protocols, regular security assessments, and continuous monitoring for unusual patterns or breaches. Additionally, fostering a culture of security awareness, where employees are trained to recognize and respond to potential threats, can greatly enhance an organization's resilience to data breaches.

Eighth, organizations should leverage data analytics to enhance clinical and operational outcomes. With an effective data governance framework in place, organizations can harness the power of analytics to gain insights that inform clinical decisions, improve patient safety, and drive operational efficiencies. Integrating business intelligence tools enables real-time data access, fostering evidence-based practices that can lead to enhanced patient experiences and reduced costs.

Ninth, fostering stakeholder engagement is crucial in maintaining an effective data governance framework. Healthcare organizations should engage patients, clinicians, and other stakeholders in discussions around data use and governance policies. Transparent communication builds trust, allowing patients to feel secure in how their data is handled, while also promoting feedback that can refine governance practices. Engaging stakeholders in data governance emphasizes a patient-centric approach that aligns data management with the goals of superior care.

Finally, organizations should regularly review and update their data governance policies and practices. Data governance is not a static endeavor; it requires ongoing assessment and adaptation to align with evolving regulations, emerging technologies, and shifting organizational needs. Regular audits and feedback loops maintain the relevance and effectiveness of governance initiatives, ensuring compliance and continuous improvement.

In conclusion, implementing a comprehensive data governance framework is non-negotiable for healthcare organizations aiming to optimize their use of health information. By adopting the recommendations outlined, organizations can create a sustainable environment where data integrity, security, and compliance are prioritized. Ultimately, these measures enhance not only operational efficiencies but also the quality of patient care, fostering a more transparent, accountable healthcare system.